PRAISE F<

It was sad that Sugar missed out on playing in the NBA, but even sadder is that the NBA missed out on Sugar and all the people who didn't get an opportunity to see him play.

— ANTHONY GORDON, INDIANA TECHNICAL INSTITUTE, SUGARMEL'S ALL-STAR TEAM

Creston's Melvin "Sugar" McLaughlin was the best pure shooter I ever saw. When he was in a zone, he'd shoot the lights out from anywhere on his side from the midcourt line. If there had been a three-point line when he was playing in the late 1970s, he would have scored a million points. If you saw him play, you'll never forget him.

— BOB BECKER, FORMER SPORTS EDITOR FOR *THE GRAND RAPIDS PRESS*

I heard about Sugar when I was growing up in Lansing. I can still picture him shooting that sweet long-range step back jumper. He is not only a Grand Rapids legend but a West Michigan treasure.

— CARL THOMAS, ASSISTANT COACH DUQUESNE UNIVERSITY, FORMER NBA PLAYER

I remember going to a game at Central Michigan. Sugar put on a show! The way he played, the excitement, and how the fans reacted. He was one reason I decided that Central Michigan would be a good place for me.

— Dan Majerle, Central Michigan Hall of Fame,
3X NBA All-Star

Melvin had that Magic-like smile. With his skill level, he'd be thriving in today's game. You didn't realize how tough and strong he was. He could get to the basket too. He wasn't just an outside shooter.

— Dave Grauzer, Central Michigan Hall of Fame,
High School Varsity Basketball Coach, Assistant

Melvin was a great competitor who could score at all three levels. He was Steph Curry playing without the three-point line.

— David Greer, Head Coach Wayne State
University, All-Time Career Assist Record
Holder Mid-American Conference (MAC)

When I played for the Knicks, only one other person could shoot from as deep as Sugar: "Downtown" Freddy Brown. I don't think anyone else can compare to him as a shooter.

— Dennis Bell, Drake University, New York
Knicks

The Jordan documentary totally reminds me of my uncle. The similarities are incredible. I was around him every day. It was AWESOME!

— Eric "Cricket" McLaughlin, Akron University
Hall of Fame, CBA

I have no doubt that Mel would have been one of the NBA's stars, especially if he had played in today's league, because you can't hand check now. He would have been impossible to guard. He's a first-class act. What I've achieved as a basketball player, he's achieved as one of our great ambassadors in the community. And that to me is a lot bigger than basketball.

— Glen Rice, 3-time NBA All-Star, NCAA and
NBA Champion

Melvin was a threat to shoot the ball by the time he passed half-court. He would still have the MAC scoring title, if they had a 3-point line when he played for Central.

— Greg Pruitt, Grand Valley State University

Sugar had no deficiencies as a ballplayer. He looked like a point guard but he was basically a scoring guard. Once he got cooking, you were going to have a long day. While most of us have retired from the game, he's never stopped playing and reaching out to the community. That speaks volumes. Skill is one thing and talent is another, but he's just a nice guy.

— JAMES MCELROY, CENTRAL MICHIGAN HALL OF FAME, NEW ORLEANS JAZZ, ATLANTA HAWKS, DETROIT PISTONS

Sugar was the "Grand Rapids Phenom." Fans packed the bleachers to see his hooping exploits. Folks would be jumping to their feet, dancing and stomping, fist pumping, and punching violently into the air. Lots of times the whole crowd would be shaking their heads at the same time in disbelief over whatever new, crazy move he just pulled on the court. I could go on and on about this Grand Rapids Hoop Hero and Legend.

— LOY VAUGHT, NCAA CHAMPION, II YEARS NBA

Sugar was so fun to watch. He could score on anybody, no matter how big. His range was so deep that guys had to pick him up just after half court. He really elevated on his mid-range jump shots and could hang in the air to finish at the rim. He is a west side legend.

— MARK HUGHES, ASSISTANT GM OF THE LOS ANGELES CLIPPERS, NCAA CHAMPION

Sugar taught me how to play the game of basketball. He's "The Man" in Grand Rapids when it comes to basketball and being a role model to look up to.

— MICHAEL "POPS" SIMS, MARQUETTE UNIVERSITY, HEAD OF THE 616 ELITE ACADEMY IN GRAND RAPIDS

We were like Bird and Magic in our mutual respect for each other. If only we had the three-point line when we played. Nobody would be able to touch our scoring records, and both us would have been in the NBA today, for sure. In my opinion, he's the best shooter to come out of the MAC, not just when we played but in its entire history. He belongs in the MAC Hall of Fame.

— RAY MCCALLUM, 1983 MAC PLAYER OF THE YEAR, ASSISTANT COACH TULANE UNIVERSITY

It was an honor to have him as a teammate. He could shoot the ball as good as Larry Bird. He just didn't get the notoriety.

— TIM BRACEY, ADIDAS HIGH SCHOOL ALL-AMERICAN-GRAND RAPIDS CRESTON, EASTERN MICHIGAN UNIVERSITY

Central Michigan's recruitment of Melvin McLaughlin was one of the great recruiting heists of all time. They saw the speed and shooting and charisma where others likely only saw the lack of size. He scored at such a level that you couldn't wait to see the acrobatic offensive arsenal the next play or next game. He electrified Rose Arena. All of us who got to watch Sugar will never forget it. He was so gifted as a player, but his personality and smile made everyone life-long fans. I know I am one.

— Tom Crean, current head coach for the University of Georgia, 2x C-USA Coach of the Year, 2003 Clair Bee Coach of the Year, 2016 Big Ten Coach of the Year

———————

For more information and to invite Vern to your school, group, church, or team, see TwigAllAmerican.com. Email him at vern.wendt@TwigAllAmerican.com

SWEET SHOT

THE BASKETBALL LIFE AND LEGACY OF MELVIN "SUGAR" MCLAUGHLIN

REV. DR. VERNON E. WENDT, JR.

TWIG ALL-AMERICAN

To my parents,
Dr. Vernon E. Wendt Sr. MD and Hildegard Wendt,
for never giving up on me,
To anyone who has ever experienced the crushing blow
of being cut from the team,
And to dreamers everywhere, young and old.

"I will pour out my Spirit on all people. Your sons
and daughters will prophesy, your old men will
dream dreams, your young men will see visions."

— JOEL 2:28

"The city streets will be filled with boys and girls
playing there."

— ZECHARIAH 8:5

FOREWORD

BY DAVE GINSBERG

Melvin "Sugar" McLaughlin's knack of finding the right shot to use at the right time was simply sensational. However, his dependable ball handling, incredible passing, and instinctive defensive prowess often went unnoticed because of his scoring. He poured chunks of points in so quickly, everyone's vision blurred as to what was actually happening in front of them! Melvin was a big-time performer—a magician with the game of basketball. His performances were mesmerizing and addictive. Those able to squeeze into arenas to watch him "show out" usually became delirious with his uniqueness.

Melvin performed at legendary levels before he ever got out of middle school in Grand Rapids, Michigan. His abilities, rare for someone so young, spoke volumes in the community. And people who loved basketball made their way into "Sugar's world" to take it all in. They were never disappointed!

Often, exceptional athletes in our society misuse their status. They take advantage of their special gifts, and become miserable, entitled people. Not so for Melvin. Sugar was loved by everyone who knew him: his family, his classmates, his coaches, teammates, and especially his army of fans. Melvin's perpetual smile was warm, genuine, and endearing. Even competitors could not quite muster up that necessary edge many athletes need in battle when facing an opponent. It was hard to get mad at Melvin! Many of our opponents told me years later that they enjoyed being in his presence and watching him "do his thing."

He was a great player with an offensive arsenal that was years ahead of its time. I've heard people say, "Melvin was Steph Curry before Steph Curry became Steph Curry!" I agree. If only the 3-point line had been in existence during Melvin's years at Central Michigan. He probably would be one of the Top Five scorers in the history of college basketball. Big statement? I believe it.

Of course, when a transcendental icon is at work, stories will follow. One of the best was Melvin's last game at Central Michigan: 6,000 people packed into the arena ninety minutes before game time. The chants began: "Beat Bird! Beat Bird! Beat Bird!" The great Larry Bird had set the arena record with 45 points a few years earlier, and the fans were demanding that Melvin "Beat Bird!" Without the 3-point rule in effect, what did Melvin score that night? 46! He probably had 14-15 baskets that would have been three-pointers. Talk about a scintillating performance!

I coached basketball for 40 beautiful seasons, 16 as an assistant at Central Michigan. I had the opportunity to be in the mix with a lot of great players, including Dan Roundfield, James McElroy, Dan Majerle, Ben Poquette, and Dave Grauzer (just to mention some of the best). I'm not sure I ever witnessed anything like what I saw during Melvin McLaughlin's four years at Central Michigan—pure magic folded up into breathtaking performances!

EPIPHANY ON THE HARDWOOD

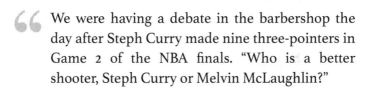 We were having a debate in the barbershop the day after Steph Curry made nine three-pointers in Game 2 of the NBA finals. "Who is a better shooter, Steph Curry or Melvin McLaughlin?"

— MEL ATKINS, SUGAR'S MIDDLE SCHOOL
BASKETBALL COACH

THE STRIPED POLE swirls its red and white colors on the post outside the door. Inside, scissors snip and click for emphasis, and words fly with equal passion as hair. Chair owners and customers contribute charged opinions in this cramped shop on the corner of Main and High Street, USA.

"I'm telling you, Steph Curry is the greatest outside shooter in the history of basketball. He's totally revolutionized how the game is played." Snip, snip, fling.

His customer swivels in the chair, in danger of losing an ear. "What about his "Splash Brother," Klay Thompson? Fourteen three-pointers in a game? Now that's revolutionary!"

"Naw. Who's the all-time leading scorer in NCAA history?"

A balding barber whisks hair from his patron's neck. "'Pistol' Pete Maravich! He didn't even play his freshman year, while averaging 44.2 points per game—before the three-point line."

Barber No. 3 lathers his customer's chin. "I'm going with James "Fly" Williams. Nearly 30 points per game at Austin Peay University from 1972-1974, from 30 feet." He grinned in the mirror at his comrades. "And his fans chanting, 'Fly is open! Let's Go Peay!'"

The lathered face challenges his knife-wielding captor. "Forget those guys. Let's talk pure shooting form! Rick "The Rocket" Mount made the cover of *Sports Illustrated*, shooting the lights out for Lebanon High School in 1966. A two-time First Team All-American at Purdue and one of the leading ABA three-point shooters."

The war rages on, from the Hoosier State, featuring Indiana State's Larry Bird and Indiana Pacers' Reggie "The Nick Killer" Miller. It ranges across the country to Jerry "Mr. Clutch" West whose image is used for the NBA logo. The impassioned hoops' aficionados chase the imaginary bouncing ball around the tiny barbershop. Voices rise and nostrils flare, as talc, lather, and dust scent the air.

"My friends, with all due respect to those mentioned and those yet to be raised, the greatest shooter of them all comes from Grand Rapids, Michigan."

Words stutter, halt, and die. All heads pivot toward the speaker, and then the voices rise again. "Grand Rapids? Can anyone good come out of Grand Rapids, Michigan?"

"If you ever saw him play, you wouldn't even ask. Melvin McLaughlin, better known as "Sugar" for his sweet game. Yes sir. Like Epiphany on the hardwood, the glory of God was shining upon him. At barely six-feet tall and 155 pounds soaking wet, Sugar radiated joy. He launched those jump shots from unprecedented range." The customer bows his head. "And he barely rippled the nets."

1

LIVING THE SWEET LIFE

> Everybody who has seen my brother play agrees that he should be a household name. But God has decided it isn't about the world, it's about Him. And He wants "Sugar Mel" to inspire the kids through these camps. This is his stage to shine on.
>
> — BOBBIE MCLAUGHLIN, MELVIN'S OLDER BROTHER

asketballs thud against hardwood. Shoes squeak as players dash about the reverberant space. I'm taking the week off from my normal responsibilities as a parish pastor in Chicago. Only I'm not in a sanctuary. I'm in the very gym of my high school archrivals, the East Kentwood Falcons located in Grand Rapids, Michigan, just outside suburban Kentwood. When I played basketball for the East Grand Rapids Pioneers, East Kentwood was the largest and most diversified high school in Kent County. It remains so today. It's also the seventh most diversified school district in the country.[1] In junior high, we played Kentwood's feeder schools, Crestwood and Valleywood Middle School. They customarily slaughtered us. The best players of both schools then went on to unite in high school, making us easy prey for the Falcons.

But I'm not in that gym to cast out the basketball playing demons of my past. Nor am I there to do penance for my substandard performances on the playing floor. Instead, I'm about to witness Melvin Sugar McLaughlin work with the kids at his annual *Sugar Mel's Sweet Shot Basketball Camp.* Sugar was the basketball player I wanted to be most like when I played in junior and senior high school.

Noisy but organized chaos ensues, registering players and distributing the correct sizes for camp shirts. After pre-camp warms-ups and chatter, camp is about to begin. A whistle pierces the din of bouncing basketballs, rubber soles on the gym floor, and a cacophony of excited voices. Bobbie McLaughlin, Sugar's older brother, is the camp director. He is both gentle and authoritative as he stops the wild free-for-all. He smiles broadly with fondness and anticipation.

Not that long ago, his little brother pleaded for such a chance to better his own ball game. Now Bobbie shoots Sugar a warm look, then summons more than 200 fifth- through eighth-grade boys and girls to join him and the staff. They hunker down at a main court basket on the south end of the gym. An equal number of high school players will arrive for the camp's afternoon session. I stand behind the basket to observe, while the campers are seated past the three-point line in a semi-circle facing the basket.

I glance at the campers' faces. Some of them may not even know where the camp's name originates! Do they realize that the figure emblazoned on the back of their new t-shirt is a depiction of him shooting his signature one-handed jump shot? A number of them may have heard stories about him from people like me, who watched him play in his prime. But our accounts may seem more like myths and old basketball tales rather than a genuine description of what really took place on the playing floor.

Hopefully these kids know what a privilege it is to attend Sugar's camp and receive the coaching advice of a living legend! As an avid basketball aficionado, I've seen a lot of players in my lifetime. I've never witnessed anyone with Sugar's ability to accurately shoot from such an extraordinary long range while under heavy pressure. He remains the greatest outside shooter I've ever seen play, including all the players I've seen on TV and via highlight films. I know Sugar would have been a star in the NBA given fairer circumstances. However, to paraphrase Ecclesiastes for basketball players: "The best shooters and the greatest players don't always make the NBA."[2]

With his winning smile, charismatic personality, good looks, and phenomenal shooting range, Sugar should be a household name, both to the kids in his hometown of Grand Rapids and to basketball fans throughout the world. Yet, rather than walk away from the sport in bitterness and self-pity, here he stands before us. He brings as much passion to his camp as if he were playing an important game. Though his personal hoop dreams didn't turn out as he'd imagined, Sugar has never soured on his love for the game of basketball.

After Bobbie's introduction, Sugar slaps a basketball enthusiastically before addressing the players for an opening pep talk. "How many of you have a desire to improve as a basketball player?" A few hands shoot into the air.

Sugar bobs his head and smiles his brilliant smile. "All the great players—Kobe, Lebron, Michael, Kyrie, Steph—had a desire to be great players. Look how well they've done. They had a love and passion for the game of basketball, and they worked their tails off to be the best. You guys can do the same thing."

Campers begin to nod in agreement, bolstered by Sugar's affirming and confident introduction. I can't help but nod along as I recall my own hoop dreams at their age; like these campers, I just knew I could be a basketball star if I worked hard enough.

Sugar says,

 "Always believe in yourself. Don't let anybody tell you that you can't do it. Don't even have the word 'can't' in your vocabulary; never say, 'I can't do that' or 'I can't do this.' Eliminate that word. Always say, 'I can' and 'I want to do this,' because you can. All right? I really want you to learn as much as you can from the staff here this week."

He directs the campers' attention to the staff standing behind him. "These guys are good at what they do, and bring with them a lot of knowledge about the game of basketball." He turns back to the campers. "I look at you, and see myself in your shoes, in your desire to be the best player possible." Sugar's gaze locks with a gangly twelve-year-old girl, tall for her age, with a determined look. "Over the years, I have learned to take the coaching advice from others and apply it to the game. That's what I did and I give credit to all those who helped me succeed in the game of basketball."

I grin. How many players get along with their coaches in junior and senior high school? I remember my frustration with coaches over my lack of playing time. "Didn't they want to win?" "Why would they bench me, when other players didn't put in half the work I had to be the best player possible?" "It wasn't fair!" Maybe if I'd heard and heeded Sugar's advice then, my so-called basketball career would have turned out differently.

Sugar's sage words continue, and the children watch him, riveted.

" But even more importantly, you can do the same in other areas of your life, as you apply the advice of your parents, relatives, teachers, pastor, and other mentors to succeed off the playing floor, as well. I don't want you to just succeed in basketball. I want you to succeed in everything you do. I don't want you to settle for just being good. I want you to be great! I want you to maximize all the gifts and talents God has blessed you with to be the best version of yourself.

This isn't a church service. However, over the years, the basketball court has not just been Sugar's sanctuary. It has become his pulpit to speak words of wisdom and advice to today's youth. "You might want to be a doctor or a teacher or a lawyer or an engineer or something else. Whatever you have a love and passion to do, do it with all your heart. Apply the advice and wisdom you receive from others. With God's help your dreams will come true in ways you can't imagine."

Some kids seem to have other dreams off the playing floor. They sit up taller, as they relate Sugar's wisdom to their life's aspirations. These words apply not only to the kids, but to myself. I'm reminded to never give up on my own God-given dreams and aspirations. With His help, they will turn out far better than we could even ask or imagine. (See Ephesians 3:20.)

Sugar concludes his opening pep talk with gratitude. "I want to thank all the coaches who are here. And your parents and guardians for bringing you here. Thank you to our sponsors for making this camp possible, and most importantly you. Thank you for being here and committing yourself over the next few days to work hard on improving your game of basketball. So, give yourself a hand!"

The campers match Sugar's excitement, clapping so loudly their hands must sting. I join in, along with the rest of the counselors. The noise is thunderous; some of the players cover their ears with their hands. Sugar's famous smile breaks out across his face, as he bellows over the pandemonium, "All right, let's start camp!"

As thrilled as I am about the impact Sugar's camp is having on the kids, I'm ecstatic to be at the camp personally to witness Sugar using his basketball gifts as a platform for outreach. Just three grades ahead of me in school, Sugar once lived three miles from me. He has the same unbridled passion for the game of basketball that I still do. Yet, we had never even talked to each other before.

Then I wrote him a letter at the beginning of 2018, asking if anyone had ever considered writing his story. A couple of months later I received a phone call from an unfamiliar number with the Grand Rapids area code. I answered, thinking it might be a spam call. Instead, a deep voice said, "I'm Bobbie McLaughlin, Sugar's brother."

He handed the phone to Sugar. I heard the smile in his greeting, "What's up, big fella?" In minutes, all three of us were swapping stories like old friends, convinced that God was at work in bringing us together.

Sugar had held on to the letter I had written, wondering if it might be legit. "Who is this Vernon Wendt Junior guy, anyway, and what's his motivation for wanting to write a book about me?" Finally, when Bobbie arrived from Los Angeles, Sugar pulled the letter from his desk. "Bro, what do you think?"

Bobbie looked up from reading the letter, beaming. "We've been praying for this!"

As a result, Sugar and I are no longer strangers. Our relationship has grown through personal interviews, interviewing others who know him, and attending his basketball camp for the last couple of years. By hanging out with him, including some shooting duels when I've visited Grand Rapids, I've come to appreciate even further not only his exceptional ability on the playing floor but also his outstanding character. Time with Sugar has elevated his status as one of the heroes God has put into my life, inspiring me to be a better person.

Every interaction since that first phone call confirms my initial impression of Melvin and Bobbie. When they visited me at my dad's house in East Grand Rapids, they arrived later than we had scheduled, delayed because Sugar was locating his scrapbook. Newspaper clippings from his storied career swelled the old binder.

When they walked up our driveway, Bobbie's smooth stride indicated a gifted athlete, and he was a bit stockier and taller than his younger brother. Sugar was dressed in sweats, and appeared to be coming from or going to a basketball game, possibly even both! He was more pigeon-toed and bow-legged than I had imagined. This really isn't all that uncommon; many top players' feet turn inward, including Michael Jordan's. An exception to the rule is Lebron James's outward feet that some have compared to a duck walk. Even more striking, however, was the size of Sugar's hands. Even though my fingers are longer than average, when he shook my hand, his hand totally dwarfed mine.

Both Bobbie and Sugar's outer appearances belie their ages. I only know Bobbie's age because he's over a decade older than Sugar. Sugar's baby face and toned basketball physique give him a youthful appearance. Time has added a few lines on his face, but when he smiles, they all come together in pleasant places. It's visible evidence of his faith and God's ability to work the detours of his basketball career for good. As David wrote in Psalm 16:6a, "The boundary lines have fallen for me in pleasant places; surely I have a delightful inheritance."

But their dignity and humility struck me the most. Having lived and served churches in Mississippi, I could tell they were raised by a southern gentleman, though they grew up in the

North. When they entered our front door, they made a point to first greet my dad, who was watching TV in the family room.

Bobbie extended his hand. "How are you doing, Doctor Wendt?" He knew instinctively how important it was for my dad to be addressed by his title. Like Sugar with basketball, my father viewed his profession as God's gift to him. Cardiology was his passion and he sought to honor God by being a loving and caring physician. He was beloved by his patients, and one of the top cardiologists in the field.

Sugar greeted him more casually, reaching out for a hand-shake. "What's up, Doc?" I was surprised they even knew my dad was a doctor. By my father's smile, I could tell he was impressed and pleased. Two strangers acknowledged him as the head of the house, and at the same time they recognized what had been his life's vocation, passion, and identity.

We made our way into the living room, followed by my curious older sister, Kathy, who had stopped by from nearby Holland, Michigan to check on our dad. When we were getting seated on the living room couch to pore over the scrapbook, Kathy asked Sugar, "So, were you a better player than Michael Jordan?"

Somewhat embarrassed, I tried to make up for my sister's bluntness. "He was a better shooter than Jordan." Sugar only laughed, though not denying my words. He had plenty he could have bragged about and could have gone into further detail about his basketball exploits. But Sugar carries a confidence that doesn't need to boast or be the center of attention. It makes him very comfortable to be around.

Before leaving, our special guests made sure to greet everyone in the house. My sister Beth had stopped by from her home a few blocks away, and her son, my nephew, Vernon Peter, was upstairs working on his computer.

And then Bobbie and Sugar made a beeline to my father, still sitting in his favorite chair in the family room. My dad's hard of hearing, making conversation difficult. Yet they managed to ask about my mom, the love of my dad's life, who had passed a couple of years earlier, along with the rest of the family. They inquired kindly about my sister Doralyn, who died unexpectedly of a rare form of cancer, months before my mother's death. Reaching out for their departing handshakes, Bobbie and Sugar both said, "Thank you, Doctor Wendt, for hosting us at your house today."

I watched them walk down our driveway to the car, Bobbie with his long strides, and Sugar with his athletic strut. I knew I was witnessing two of God's royal children in action, the McLaughlin brothers of Grand Rapids. There may not have been any fanfare or media coverage, but the person I looked up to growing up and his older brother had just visited my boyhood home. Even now, Bobbie and Sugar regularly ask me how my dad is doing. And even though my dad has severe dementia these days, he still inquires about Sugar and Bobbie. They left an impression that isn't easily forgotten.

Viewing the hoopla at camp from my spot near the basket, I remember the first time I saw Sugar play. He was a senior in high school and I was a freshman. Later, I watched him wow the crowd at the "Center Court" (aka, the McNeal driveway) of the Gus Macker 3 on 3 Tournaments in Lowell, Michigan. In addition to his almost supernatural playing ability, Sugar had another particular quality I admired. He personified my definition of coolness in the late 70s and early 80s. It was a time for breaking down racial barriers in America politically and culturally. Though I grew up in mostly white suburban East Grand Rapids, while Sugar grew up in a predominantly black neighborhood in inner city Grand Rapids, we shared a common love for an orange ball.

During the 90s the famous Gatorade commercial implied that its consumers "wanted to be like Mike." Similarly, in the 70s and 80s I sure wanted to be like Sugar. I continued to follow

Sugar and his basketball playing feats in *The Grand Rapids Press* and the *Detroit Free Press*. Years later I added his name to my Google alerts. I bragged to others that the best basketball player I ever saw came from my hometown of Grand Rapids. A frequent response was "Melvin who?" and a skeptical look, as if I were either putting them on, crazy, or both.

Sugar Mel's Sweet Shot Basketball Camp begins by choosing a boy and a girl to shoot a free throw, followed by Sugar. According to tradition, camp cannot start until all three of them make a free throw. The twelve-year-old girl Sugar had locked eyes with earlier is chosen, along with a boy of the same age, a starting guard for Crestwood Middle School. She receives a pass from Sugar, then confidently steps to the line. She dribbles four times. She cocks the ball with her right wrist and spreads her fingers. She bends her legs, and pushes the ball upwards towards the goal. The ball slides through the net. Sugar, the coaches, the campers, and those of us on the sidelines erupt with shouts of encouragement. Excited, she retrieves the ball and executes a crisp pass, chest high, into the waiting hands of her rival, shouting, "Next!"

Taking up the challenge, the eighth-grade star swaggers to the line. "Take notes!" he says. He defiantly bounces the ball a couple of times, aims, and shoots. *Clang!* His line drive shot hits the back of the rim. Taunts burst from the crowd: "Brick!" "Don't break the rim!" "You forgot to go to McDonald's this morning! You need to get some arch on that shot!" "Maybe you should try a 'Rick Berry' and shoot granny style!" He rolls his eyes and chases down his errant shot, then moves to the line again, unshaken. This time, he bounces the ball twice, aims, and shoots a perfectly formed set shot. "Yes!" He pumps his fists triumphantly in the sky, silencing his critics.

Sugar then steps up to the line. He eyes the basket, bounces the ball once, and launches his sling-shot style shot from behind his head. It barely rustles the net.

The camp can now officially begin.

Since the early 1990s, Sugar and Bobbie have been serving Grand Rapids' area youth through their camp. It is the longest running, affordable, non-profit basketball camp in West Michigan. Through the support of local businesses, Sugar makes certain that no children are turned away because they can't afford to attend.

The fundamentals of basketball act as a bridge. They communicate in a fun, meaningful, and effective way the necessary skills for a successful life. "We stress to the kids that it's not just basketball," Bobbie, the camp's director, states.

 Basketball teaches life concepts. For instance, you want to take that assist part, helping one another, assisting one another, from the gym to the home to the world. Take it to your family. Learn to work together, play together. That whole concept is what we teach these kids, along with basic skills and fundamentals. It's a long learning process, and you want to learn that and keep it going outside of basketball camp, too.

Other life skills bridged at the camp include:

Discipline: From the opening of the camp, the players are in constant motion. There is little standing around and nobody wastes time waiting their turn. Players are being taught the discipline of diligence in order to achieve their goals.

Faithfulness: Don't expect others to do things for you. Faithfully fulfill your own role. The players are taught basic offensive and defensive schemes, and learn the importance of faithfully carrying out their individual roles to achieve success.

Responsibility: Don't blame others for your mistakes. Acknowledge your wrongs and seek to make up for them.

Players are taught to openly admit their individual defensive and offensive lapses. Correspondingly, they are encouraged to make up for these mistakes the next time down the court.

Community: They learn to compete on the basketball floor, while having fun at the same time. The campers work together and contribute to the success of their community. Camp teams are formed of players who typically have never teamed with each other. During camp, they learn to work with their teammates along with their assigned coach.

Always Strive to Do Your Best: Don't settle for just being good enough. Be willing to make the sacrifices needed in order to be great both on and off the court. Throughout the camp, counselors push the players by challenging them: "Is that the best you can do?" "Are you trying your hardest?" They can apply these questions to all areas of their lives.

Gazing at these students, I do the math: all these years multiplied by hundreds of kids then multiplied by all their family, friends, and future contacts. The ripple effect is humbling. Melvin Sugar McLaughlin may not be considered rich or famous in the eyes of the world. His wealth and acclaim come from his investment in the countless lives of his campers. His dream will result in their traveling not the broad road leading to destruction, but the road of success.

Because of his annual basketball camps, Sugar is more popular than ever. Recently, a twenty-something guy approached him in the grocery store. "You don't remember me," he said, "but I came to your camp in sixth grade. It was the most significant time of my life. You inspired me." And that emphasizes the new spin on Sugar's original dream.

"A word of encouragement can change someone's day—or life. Words are powerful," he says. "Kids finding their gifts gives hope; they can have something to really live for. If they see a positive person in front of them, sharing their own stories of hard work and achievement...their mindset is 'I can do that too.'"

Though he didn't make the NBA as he dreamed, Sugar has found contentment. He knows he is in the place and position where God wants him to be.

In the long run, his hoop dreams have turned out to be as sweet as his game on the playing floor. Sugar is indeed living the sweet life.

TWO SOON, TWO LATE

> Sugar was a great player, light years ahead of his time. Today, he would be the most valuable player on your team, with the value of the 3-point shot. Our league is all about the math now and his style of play affects the math of winning and points per possession. Three points add up faster than two! He might have had a different career if the 3-point line was perceived as valuable then as it is now.
>
> — JIMMY BOYLEN, NBA CHAMPIONSHIP COACH

Had Sugar been born at a later date in time, his childhood dream of NBA stardom would have had a much better chance of turning out as he imagined. But in God's providence, Sugar was born in 1960. Hence, when he tried out for the NBA in 1983, he wasn't given the same chance to play in the league as he would have had today. Shooting a basket from extraordinarily long distances would make Sugar a highly sought-after player in today's NBA, where the three-point play has become an essential part of the game.

The NBA introduced the three-point play in the 1979-1980 season, when Sugar was a freshman in college. At the time it was considered more or less a gimmick. Bill Simmons in *The Book of Basketball* contends that it took eight years for the 3-point shot to fully establish itself in the NBA. Several events led to this breakthrough. First, Larry Bird won the first three-point contest at All-Star weekend, after guaranteeing his victory beforehand. He then adopted the three as a weapon in regular season play, helping Boston win the 1986 NBA championship.

Then several three-point specialists emerged. Craig Hodges (45%), Trent Tucker (44%), Kyle Macy (41%), Michael Cooper (39%), and Dale Ellis (36%), spread the floor and opened up things for their teammates down low. Other clinchers were some particularly memorable three-pointers that year. When Jeff Malone chased down a loose ball and fell out of bounds while making a three, they showed it in "the NBA....It's FANNNNtastic" commercials over a solid year.[1]

Danny Ainge was arguably the first player to prove that the 3-point shot could be an integral part of a championship contender's offense, breaking the previous record of 92 3-pointers with 148 threes for Coach K.C. Jones's 1987-1988 Boston Celtics. In the late 1980s and early 1990s, 5-foot-10 Michael Adams of the Denver Nuggets led the league, launching the most three-point attempts with his push shot. The three-point shot then jumped from 10 attempts per game to 15 when the NBA experimented with a uniform 22 feet from the basket from 1994 to 1997. John Starks broke the 200 barrier in the 1994-1995 season, making 217 three-point shots out of 611 attempts.

After the three-point line reverted to its present distance of 23'9" (22' at the corners) in the 1997-1998 season, the pace slowed briefly. Seattle Supersonics Ray Allen would go on to set a record of 269 three-pointers in 2005-2006.

Then along came Stephen Curry. Given their similar styles of play, he and Sugar are most commonly compared with one another. Curry led the Golden State Warriors to NBA Championships in 2015, 2017, and 2018. He revolutionized the game with his volume and efficiency from the three-point line. In his debut season, 2009-2010, he made 166 three-pointers, the most ever by a rookie. But his breakout season was in 2012-13, when he smashed the record with 272. He led the league the next four seasons, surpassing this total three times, including the current season record of 402 in 2015-2016. In October of 2016, Curry became the fastest player to reach 1600 career-made three-pointers. The following season, in December of 2017, Steph became the fastest player to reach 2000 career treys. In Game 1 of the 2019 NBA conference finals, he matched his post-season career high, loading nine three-pointers in a win over the Portland Trail Blazers. He previously had made nine three-pointers in the 2018 NBA playoffs in Game 1 of the conference finals.

But even if Steph Curry had never picked up a basketball, the 3-point record would have eventually tumbled. His teammate Klay Thompson, the Rockets' James Harden (who led the league in three-point shots in 2017-2018 with 265 and in 2018-2019 with 378), and Portland's Damian Lillard, are among the top three-point servers in today's league. They're pouring in three-pointers at rates that would have astounded the players, fans, and coaches of the early 1980s.

The 1980 cynics of the 3-point play have been proven wrong. The "beyond the arc" shot has evolved from a gimmick used when a team is desperate to catch up from far behind. Instead, it's an essential part of today's game. Teams quickly figured out that the bonus of an extra point gives them a better chance of winning games.

Consequently, the value of being able to shoot from long range is higher than ever in the history of basketball. Gregory "Special K" Kelser teamed up with Magic Johnson to win the 1979 NCAA Championship and played in the NBA from 1979-

1985. Kelser, the current commentator for the Detroit Pistons games on Fox Sports Detroit says,

 At the time when Melvin played and came out of college, it was not a shot that was used the way it is today. Now it's the dominant shot in the game. It has totally eroded the significance of a middle range game. Guys are either right at the basket or they're out beyond the arc. He could have thrived in an era like right now, as a special weapon.

On the other hand, a sooner-born Sugar could have starred in the former American Basketball Association. The ABA, a men's professional basketball league, began in 1967 and eventually merged with the NBA in 1976. It distinguished itself from its older counterpart with a more wide-open, flashy style of offensive play. There were also different rules, such as a 30-second shot clock as opposed to the NBA's 24-second clock. The ABA switched to the 24-second clock for its final season in 1975-1976.

But the main difference, as far as Sugar's outside shooting prowess is concerned, was the ABA's usage of a three-point field goal arc. Along with the slam dunk, the ABA used the shot to create excitement during the game, and to differentiate itself from the NBA. The ABA's first commissioner was George Mikan. He had usurped the three-point shot and its distance from the defunct American Basketball League (1960-1961). Sometimes referred to as a "25-foot shot," when measured, the line was actually 23 feet and nine inches from the key area. The corner shots were 22 feet. As Mikan reflected, "We called it the home run because the three-pointer was exactly that. It brought fans out of their seats."[2]

The NBA focused primarily on the sound but often dull fundamentals of the game. In contrast, the ABA was like a professional playground for street-ballers where they could display their unique individual skills. The NBA was more of a symphony, with script set-plays. In contrast, the ABA was like a jazz concert, where players were encouraged to improvise and go with the flow. The players would feel something and try it. Afterward, fans and sometimes the players themselves were not even sure what they'd done! Their eye-catching red, white, and blue colored basketball only added to the ABA's flashiness.

The league featured some of the game's most flamboyant players in Julius "Dr. J." Irving, David "Skywalker" Thompson, and George "The Iceman" Gervin. The ABA's freewheeling style eventually caught on with the fans. But lack of a national television contract and financial hardships led to its eventual demise. By the time Sugar came out of Central Michigan in 1983, the ABA was defunct.

As Sugar postulates,

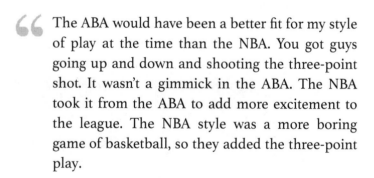

> The ABA would have been a better fit for my style of play at the time than the NBA. You got guys going up and down and shooting the three-point shot. It wasn't a gimmick in the ABA. The NBA took it from the ABA to add more excitement to the league. The NBA style was a more boring game of basketball, so they added the three-point play.

But even in the "running and gunning" ABA, teams shot from long range only an occasional five or six times per game. In today's NBA, teams shoot from behind the arc an average of 30-40 times per game. Consequently, Sugar says, "The game has changed tremendously from 35 years ago to now. I look at my game as being ahead of its time because way back then, I was playing the way they are now. Back then, they didn't have the 3-point line in high school or college. I missed out. I guess timing is everything."[3]

In the Bible, Esther's outward beauty resulted in her becoming the Queen of Persia. Mordecai wisely says to his niece, "And who knows but that you have come to your royal position for such a time as this?" (Esther 4:14). Born sooner, Esther would have been an old woman and not considered a fitting candidate for King Xerxes' wife. On the other hand, had Esther been born at a later time, she would have been a little girl and not ready to be a queen. Instead, God raised her up at a particular time in history to use her influence as the Queen of Persia to rescue His people.

Similarly, Sugar might have been a rich and famous professional basketball player if he had been born later and tried out for today's NBA, or possibly in the ABA if he had been born sooner. But he realizes that the Giver of all Good Gifts has also determined the time and place in which to use these gifts. As a result, God has given him the gift of basketball to influence others as a player, teammate, and community member, "for such a time as this." Literally thousands of young lives have been impacted over the years through Sugar Mel's Sweet Shot Basketball Camp, not only resulting in better basketball players, but above all, better people.

For over two decades Ottawa Hills High School in Grand Rapids hosted the camp. Sugar and Bobbie are especially thankful for Marcus Harris, the athletic director of Ottawa Hills. Further, the rest of the Ottawa Hills' staff has been exceptionally supportive over the years. Due to its growing popularity, the camp has relocated to East Kentwood High School. The Falcons' more spacious facility is able to accommodate more campers. As with Ottawa Hills, Bobbie and Sugar really appreciate how the East Kentwood Public Schools' superintendent Michael Zoerhoff, East Kentwood High School's principal Omar Bakri, and the rest of the East Kentwood staff have come through in supporting their camp and its campers.

One former camper started out younger than most. His dad,

Craig, asked if it was possible for Drew, who was about to enter the fourth grade, to register for camp. He insisted, "He's really good for his age." However, the camp is intended for players entering the fifth through twelfth grades.

Anthony Gordon, Crestwood Middle School's athletic director, recalls his dilemma. In spite of the father's insistence, he wasn't sure if he should allow the underaged player to attend the camp. Not wanting to be seen as the bad guy, he responded, "Let me ask Bobbie if it would be okay. He's the camp director."

Bobbie affirmed their camp's goal: to turn away no kid who desires to attend. He told Craig, "The camp is really not meant for fourth graders, but let's see what he can do."

Drew, naturally carrying a basketball, showed off some ball-handling skills in the hallway, as proof that he was up for the challenge. Sugar took note. He could relate to the father-son plight, after not getting a chance in his professional tryouts. He backed his brother with an encouraging nod. "Yeah, let's see what he can do."

That week Drew won the free-throw shooting contest, the three-point shot contest, and the one-on-one contest. The youngest kid in the camp took home three personal trophies all because Bobbie and Sugar had given him a chance. Drew Neitzel would become Michigan's Mr. Basketball in 2004. He averaged 32.7 points and 8.9 assists per game in leading Wyoming Park High School to the final four in the Class B State Tournament. They eventually lost to nationally ranked Detroit Renaissance in their closest game of the year. He would go on to play for the Michigan State Spartans, scoring 1534 points and making 582 assists. After playing a couple of years professionally in Europe, Drew settled back down in Grand Rapids. Following in Sugar's footsteps, he holds an annual summer basketball camp for players ranging from third through eighth grade. The Drew Neitzel Basketball Camp is held at the Courthouse Athletic Center of Grand Rapids.

Neitzel hasn't been the only exception to the rule. St. Paul advised Timothy not to look down upon others because of their youth (1 Timothy 4:12). And Jesus insisted that no one should prevent little children from receiving His blessing (Matthew 19:14). Similarly, Bobbie and Sugar maintain that no child should be barred from being blessed by their camp. It's not unusual for them to lower the camp's age limit bar for younger players to attend. The upstarts are welcomed with the challenge, "Let's see what you can do!"

An outstanding alumna of Sugar's camp is Presley Hudson, of Wayland High School. Presley attended the camp as a middle schooler. She went on to eclipse Sugar's scoring record of 2071 points at Central Michigan University with 2309 career points. Sugar is proud of the connection she has with the camp, as well as her being a fellow Chippewa.[4] After being cut from the WNBA's Seattle Storm before the 2019 season, Presley signed to play with the basketball team Politechnika Gdańska in Gdansk, Poland. Presley also has worked as a coach at Drew Neitzel's Basketball Camp in the past.

Besides Neitzel and Presley, additional camp alumni have gone on to play college basketball. JaKarri Alven and Miryah Barnes played for Aquinas College, Cleveland "CJ" Baskin for Lake Michigan College, and Markus Bingham for Michigan State University. Others include Alona Blackwell (Oakland University), Kobe Bufkin (University of Michigan), BJ Comer (TLAP Sports Academy), Jordan Jackson (Wilmington University), Ja'Moni Jones (Schoolcraft College), and Hayden Large (Dordt University). A number of former campers chose to focus on other sports for their college athletic careers.

Sugar's niece Tami prays that someday a player at her uncle's camp will grow up to play in the NBA or WNBA. This would be visible evidence of just what an impact the camp has had on all those who have attended. But whether the campers become star basketball players or not, the main goal of camp is that everyone knows how important and unique they are in the eyes of God. They are inspired to follow their dreams of success both on and off the playing floor by "Daring to be Great."

As the campers state, squaring their shoulders and standing straight and proud, "If Sugar can do it, I can too."

3

CALL HIM SUGAR

> Sugar should be my first name. No one ever calls me Melvin. If someone calls me Melvin, it's either my family or I'm in trouble.
>
> — MELVIN "SUGAR" McLAUGHLIN

Born to Bobbie and Mary Ruth McLaughlin, Melvin was the youngest of their four children. In addition to his brother Bobbie (aka "Junior"), who was twelve years older than him, Melvin had two older sisters. Patricia Veronica was a year older than Bobbie, and Gracie a year younger than Bobbie.

Melvin's last name has been both a source of confusion and humor over the years. For example, one time, he was out to eat with his brother Bobbie, and they wrote their family name on a waiting list to be called for seating.

One of the hosts eventually called out, "The McLaughlin party!" Bobbie and Melvin both stood in response, ready to follow him to their seats. But when the host saw them get up, he asked, "Can I help you?"

"Yeah, you just called the McLaughlin party, and we're the McLaughlins." Bobbie laughs telling the story. "I wish I had a camera, because he realized his mistake and couldn't do anything about it. All he could do was say, 'Oh, my goodness! I'm sorry. I blew it!'"

Bobbie and Melvin genially assured him, "We're all good, bro. Don't worry about it."

Ron Sendre was the head athletic trainer at Central Michigan when Melvin played for the Chippewas. He jokingly nicknamed Melvin "Irish," following a call by former University of Nevada at Las Vegas (UNLV) coach Jerry Tarkanian. Central Michigan had been scheduled to play UNLV, but a scheduling conflict postponed their matchup. Tarkanian called to apologize to CMU's head coach at the time, Dick Parfitt. Parfitt graciously agreed to schedule a game between the two schools at a later date. Tarkanian had witnessed Melvin play in a high school All-Star game in Ohio. Afterward he recruited him heavily for his Runnin' Rebels. Before he hung up, he said in jest, "Hey, I heard you got that Irish kid, Melvin McLaughlin, playing for your team. He's a pretty good little player, isn't he?" Ever since, Sendre, who overheard Tarkanian's call on speaker phone, customarily greets Sugar by saying, "Hey, Irish!" Sugar routinely responds, "Hey, Angelo!" based upon the name of Muhammad Ali's legendary trainer, Angelo Dundee.

The McLaughlin name can be traced to his dad's father, Ira, also known as Mack. Ira was born in 1855 in Carthage, Mississippi, the son of a black slave. The white overseer who fathered Ira is commonly referred to as "The Irishman" in family lore. Bobbie Senior's mother, Georgia Sanders, was part black and part Choctaw Indian and was born in 1881. Her family lived near an Indian reservation and she married Mack when she was just thirteen years old.[1]

Bobbie recalls the impact of the TV mini-series *Roots*, when it was first broadcast in 1977. Author Alex Haley also traced his roots to an Irish family, only with the last name Murray. "When I saw that, it brought tears to my eyes. It gave me more understanding and a deeper appreciation of where we came from as McLaughlins. You're not going to go to Africa and see a McLaughlin tribe."

According to the web site MyNameStats.com, less than seven percent of people in the United States with the last name of McLaughlin are black.[2] So when the family meets a black person named McLaughlin, they figure they're somehow related.

Mary Ruth McLaughlin named her youngest child Melvin, a name with roots in Ireland. In Celtic, Melvin meant "chief" and in Irish it meant "leader." Although the reason she chose to name her youngest son Melvin had nothing to do with harmonizing the origins of his first and last names. She chose Melvin simply because she liked the name.

Mary Ruth insisted that Melvin be called by his given name. One day Bobbie referred to his baby brother as "that boy." She jumped all over him for not calling him Melvin. "I got in trouble for calling him that. I think I mentioned something like, 'You gotta stop that boy from crying like that.' She said, 'Don't say that. He's not That Boy! His name is Melvin!' And I'm like 'Okay! Melvin it is, then.' I'll never forget that."

Even though his mother was insistent that her youngest child be called Melvin, eventually he would become more commonly known to others as Sugar.

Melvin picked up his nickname Sugar while playing for Alexander Elementary School in fifth or sixth grade. After school, he and his friends used to go to the Baxter Community Center. The rec center still exists on the southeast side of Grand Rapids.

An after-school director, George Knighton, is credited for giving Melvin his iconic nickname. The 6'7" Knighton had been a standout player for New Mexico State from 1959-1962, where he had a double-double average (21.1 ppg, 11.5 rpg).[3] He ended up playing for the Grand Rapids Tackers, a popular local basketball team. The Tackers played in various semi-professional leagues from 1961-1974. Knighton supplemented his income by working at the Baxter Community Center. At the same time, this gave him an opportunity to give back to the community by working with the youth.

Sugar still recalls getting his nickname from Knighton, while playing in a game at the Center. "I was coming down, doing a move, between my legs, behind my back, and took a long jump shot. It went in, and George was watching. He said, 'That move was sweet as sugar. I'm going to start calling you Sugar.' It stuck from that point on."[4]

Granville Brown, former head basketball coach for the Grand Rapids Junior College Raiders (1990-1992), co-founded the TA-WA-SI All-Star Games. Brown reveals that a comic strip was named after Melvin when he was in middle school. Robert Gill, an educator and artist for *The Grand Rapids Press*, maintained that every newspaper should carry at least one comic strip by a minority artist that prominently featured minority characters.[5] Gill created a strip highlighting the humor and sweetness of black family life, naming it "Sugar" after a sweet-shooting middle schooler known by the same moniker. The strip ran from 1973 to 1999, ending with Gill's death. As Brown discloses, "A lot of people don't know that Gill named his strip after Sugar."

When fans watched him play in middle and high school, a common chant could be heard throughout the gym on both sides: "Shoot it, Sug!" Prior to Mel's senior year at Central Michigan University, Gene Church was Central's Publications Office Manager. He and Fred Stabley, Jr., Sports Information Director, were brainstorming how to promote Sugar for the national All-American team. Stabley suggested sugar cubes to help hype Melvin's candidacy. Church responded, "Why not sugar packets?" And so for $90, Church ordered sugar packets from the Gordan Food Company in Grand Rapids. Each packet featured Sugar's face, with his achievements listed on the back. Stabley used the packets in his correspondence to other schools and the media, informing them about Central Michigan's All-American contender. Those sugar packets drew calls and responses from across the U.S.

Sugar didn't make the All-American team. But Church was rewarded nationally by the Council for Advancement and Support of Education. The sugar packet was one of 22 Exceptional Achievement winners selected among 737 entries.[6] Chippewa alumni and fans still talk fondly about Church's "Melvin Sugar Packet" promotion of their sharp shooting star.

When he formed his basketball camp, Melvin chose the name Sugar Mel's, a combination of his nickname and given name. Some younger campers have never heard of or met Sugar before. They may wonder if the camp is named after a cereal on par with Sugar Pops™ and Sugar Smacks™. Bobbie laughs, imagining an uninformed camper asking, "Who is Sugar Mel? Is that a cereal? Can I get it at the grocery store?"

While family members and close friends still call him Melvin or just Mel for short, to everyone else he's known as Sugar. And even though he was never given a middle name, when asked for his middle name, Melvin responds, "It's Sugar!"

Still, based upon how often people call him by his signature nickname, Sugar might as well be his first, middle, and last names. Not only does it fit his playing style, but it also fits his demeanor both on and off the playing floor. Though he has the playing ability of a big-time star, you'd never guess it when you're around him. He doesn't put on airs or brag about himself. Instead, he remains humble and approachable to people of all ages and backgrounds. "Jumping" Jack Kelly played for Creston High School in the 1980s and is considered one of the greatest street ball dunkers of all time. At the Gus Macker 45th Anniversary Banquet, Kelly emphasized to me, "Everybody loves Sugar!"

Michael Brown worked with Melvin at Sigsbee Park. He observes, "When some people hear the name Sugar, they think of (the boxers) Ray Robinson or Leonard. People from Western Michigan's first thoughts are of our own Sugar Mel."

4

LOVE AT FIRST BOUNCE

> I still have the same kind of passion and love for the game of basketball, like it was yesterday, like I had when I was growing up as a kid, like I had when I was in middle school, like I had when I was in high school and like I had when I was in college. People recognize me for that. That will be a part of my legacy.
>
> — SUGAR MCLAUGHLIN

God instilled in Sugar a love and passion for the game of basketball when he was just four years old. In fact, in 1964, his love for that orange ball was so great that he almost lost his life because of it.

When the McLaughlin family still lived in Ann Arbor, their house was located on Main Street. Main Street was a heavily traveled thoroughfare in and out of the city. Their gravel driveway had a sloping incline. Bobbie, around sixteen at the time, created a makeshift basketball hoop. He cut the bottom out of a peach basket so he and his little brother could shoot in their backyard. One day, their parents were saying good-bye to some visiting relatives. The basketball the brothers were playing with started to roll from their backyard. It went down the hill of their front yard driveway. The ball picked up momentum, moving at a pretty good clip by the time it crossed the highway. Fortunately, the ball rolled across the highway without being hit by any cars.

Bobbie chased it down and grabbed it. Seeing Bobbie holding the basketball, Sugar tore after it with reckless abandon, thinking, "I gotta get that ball! I'm going to get that ball no matter what!"

His parents and relatives frantically chased after Sugar, trying to grab him. Panicked, they yelled, "Stop running before you get hit by a car." He didn't slow down. "Stop him!" They shouted to no one and everyone. "Somebody, grab him before it's too late!"

Everyone scrambled, equally frantic. "I can't! He's too fast!"

Sugar was so focused on going after the basketball, he wasn't easily stopped. Even then, he demonstrated an elusiveness that would become part of his playing style on the basketball court. He ran so fast on the gravel driveway that he started slipping and sliding. But rough terrain did not deter him. He had to get that basketball.

Bobbie saw a potential tragedy unfolding. Without intervention, Sugar's momentum would certainly carry him onto the busy street to be hit by a moving car. All the family members and relatives shouting from the other side knew this, as well.

Bobbie felt helpless. There seemed to be nothing he could do, so he cried out, "Oh, God, help me!" God answered Bobbie's prayer by inspiring him to do the only thing he could do to stop his little brother from potentially losing his life. He threw the rescued basketball at Sugar with the intention of hitting him full on. Bobbie, an outstanding outfielder at the time, applied his baseball skills by successfully hurling a perfect strike at his little brother's chest. His bright grin flashes. "Never in all my baseball playing days have I thrown a ball that accurately."

The hit stopped Sugar in his tracks. He slid and fell down at the far end of the driveway. Cars in front of him swerved to avoid hitting him. Sugar had been spared from being hit by a car. Their dad's reaction was simultaneously angry and happy. He was angry that his youngest child could have lost his life chasing after a basketball. At the same time, he was happy. For the potential death of his son running into the street and being run over by a car had been thwarted.

Since he was so young, Sugar only vaguely remembers the incident. But Bobbie has always reminded him of how his life was spared that day. God has a reason for him to be alive. Sugar does remember everyone yelling at him and trying to stop him. Nevertheless, he was determined to get the basketball that his brother Bobbie held on the other side of the street. "All I was thinking about was the ball! I had to get that ball! That was my introduction to the game of basketball."

Bobbie adds, "It was a scary introduction at that! I got scolded. He got scolded! He was crying. Out of fear and anger, my dad said, 'Give me the ball and don't ever play with it again!'" Bobbie continues,

 But we got through it. I'm convinced that God intervened for me to hit him like that, so he didn't run into the street. I had no other option. He had eluded everybody who had been reaching for him. The only thing I could think of was to hit him with the ball and knock him down. Sure enough, I threw a bullet to his chest, and bam, knocked him down. Even though it had been a scary introduction to the game of basketball, it was like a God Thing that had been instilled in him.

In his collection of essays, *All Things Considered*, G. K. Chesterton expresses, "Earth is a taskmaster and heaven is a playground," based upon the restored Kingdom of God described in Zechariah 8:5, "The city streets will be filled with boys and girls playing there." Play, then, can be seen as a type of heaven. Basketball really can be a God Thing.

In this sense, playing sports can be considered recreational by expressing the new creation God has prepared for His people in heaven. Consequently, a case can be made that Sugar has found a foretaste of heaven on earth in basketball. Perhaps that explains his insatiable love for the game. He's been chasing the ball ever since, resolute to participate regardless of the obstacles, including traveling cars on the street.

From that point on, he always wanted a basketball in his possession. His niece, Tami, recalls, "You didn't even dare to try to take the ball away from him, or else!" When family members and friends wanted to find him, all they had to do was look for him at the nearest playground or basketball court, where he would be passionately working on improving his game.

At the park, even when it got dark, he would keep on shooting, listening for the swoosh of the metal chain net to assure him that he was on target. More than once he came home from the park at night, climbing a ladder and slipping into his upstairs bedroom to avoid a spanking from his father for coming home after dark.

Michigan winters mean cold and snow. To get his shots in, Sugar shoveled the snow off the court. Sometimes he bribed his nephews and nieces with hot chocolate afterwards as a reward for retrieving his shots. He would become an almost permanent fixture in the gyms and parks, shooting a minimum of 500 shots a day.

Growing up, Sugar also played baseball and football. With his speed and dexterity, he excelled in gridiron, or non-contact, football. However, his dad wisely persuaded him to hang up his cleats due to his slight body frame. He looked up to his older brother Bobbie and sought to emulate him as a baseball player. But basketball magnetized him in such a way that he was reluctant to pull away from playing hoops even for a season. Basketball soon became his singular focus as a sport. To paraphrase Philippians 2:13, "God had worked in Sugar both the desire and ability to play basketball for his good pleasure."

The same love and passion that God instilled in him for basketball at four-and-a-half is just as unquenchable today, over fifty years later. While most of his contemporaries long ago hung up their basketball shoes, Sugar remains obsessed with the game. He still frequents the gyms and playgrounds of Grand Rapids daily, customarily playing up to three to four hours. For Sugar, his day job is just a way to put money on the table rather than his true passion. As soon as he gets out of work, he heads for the basketball courts, occasionally explaining to others, "I gotta get my cardio in!" Craig Neitzel marvels, "It's amazing that he's still doing what he's doing every day on the basketball court at his age."

Bennette Gay played with Sugar at Creston High School as a senior when Sugar was a sophomore. He eventually became one of Sugar's closest friends. He emphasizes, "Nobody I know loves basketball more than Mel. I thought I loved basketball until I met him." Linda Chandler, who met Sugar in high school and has been the main woman in his life ever since, agrees. "Basketball is Melvin's life."

In contrast to Sugar, there are plenty of players who don't really love the sport of basketball. They mainly play because they're good at it. They might jump higher than others, shoot the ball with uncanny accuracy, or be blessed with superior height and foot speed. Still others see basketball as simply a means to an end. The round ball can help them earn a college scholarship or make a living by playing professionally. Sugar, however, truly loves basketball both intrinsically and altruistically and views it as a gift from God to him.

Just like when he was growing up, if you want to find him today, search the gyms and parks in and around Grand Rapids. You'll soon find him getting his shots in, and demonstrating a move to an up-and-coming player. Or else playing a pick-up game, while challenging others in a shooting contest. As he says with his infectious grin, "I still go out there and show the younger guys how it's done. I love it. I'm a baller for life."[1]

But perhaps the greatest joy that he has found as a seasoned citizen of the hardwood, is reaching out to the young lives in the community, particularly through his annual Sugar Mel Sweet Shot basketball camps. Consequently, he gives thanks and praise to God for blessing him with his ability to play basketball. That gift has positioned him to give back to the community.

5

FUN, LAUGHTER, AND MUSIC IN ANN ARBOR

66 My mom was a good person—very funny and lovable. She loved music. I wish Melvin had gotten a chance to know her better.

— BOBBIE MCLAUGHLIN

F un, laughter and music filled Sugar's growing up years in Ann Arbor. An uncle ran a laundry and dry-cleaning business in Ann Arbor, so Sugar's dad joined him in order to make a living. But Bobbie McLaughlin Senior also dabbled in the music business, thanks to his younger brother, Ollie.

In the late forties, Ollie McLaughlin moved to Ann Arbor to become a disc jockey for Huron River Valley station WHRV. (In 1963, new owners would change the station to WAAM, short for Ann Arbor, Michigan.) His nightly program, "Ollie's Caravan," became a fixture at WHRV almost as soon as it aired in 1952. Eric Carpenter, a student at the University of Michigan from 1953 to 1957, recalls, "Ollie had a very special voice. He had the perfect voice for a DJ, and he had the kind of program format that played the music that appealed to both the secular and collegiate audience."[1]

Sugar's Uncle Ollie eventually founded what he called the Scooby Doo Club. It's not clear why Ollie McLaughlin chose the name. The animated television show featuring a talking Great Dane had yet to be created. Ollie's son and Sugar's cousin, Ira, conjectures that it might have come from the saying, "You're a real cool Scooby Doo." It implied that you were a cool person.[2] In the decade that birthed rock and roll, being cool was vitally important. The worst thing to happen to you was to be considered uncool and a square. Ollie McLaughlin optimistically believed that everyone could be a Real Cool Scooby Doo. Over 10,000 members would ultimately join the club. In order to be a member, you only had to listen to Ollie and make a pledge to try to be nice to others. As quaint as that may sound, being a member of the Scooby Doo Club was massive to the young people in Ann Arbor in the 50s and early 60s. Dale Leslie, a former marketing director of the Ann Arbor Chamber of Commerce, was a proud member of the Scooby Doo Club. He points to Ollie as a marketing wiz.

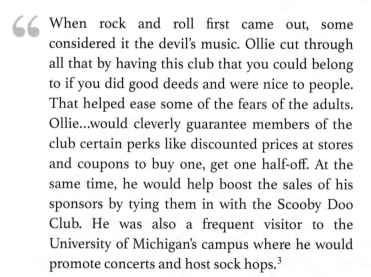

> When rock and roll first came out, some considered it the devil's music. Ollie cut through all that by having this club that you could belong to if you did good deeds and were nice to people. That helped ease some of the fears of the adults. Ollie...would cleverly guarantee members of the club certain perks like discounted prices at stores and coupons to buy one, get one half-off. At the same time, he would help boost the sales of his sponsors by tying them in with the Scooby Doo Club. He was also a frequent visitor to the University of Michigan's campus where he would promote concerts and host sock hops.[3]

Sammy Kaplan got to know Sugar's uncle on campus during the 1950s. He says, "Ollie played rock and roll and took dedications Monday through Friday. He had a huge following among the U of M students. Ollie did a lot of one-nighters, record hops, and shows, and he was very popular among his listening audience."[4]

In addition to being a DJ, Ollie was a jazz concert promoter and a music publisher. As a talent scout, he discovered both Del Shannon and Barbara Lewis. He was also a record producer, owning three important Michigan record labels that he named after his daughters, Carla, Karen, and Moira (Sugar's cousins). These labels contain some of the smoothest, slickest soul to come out of Detroit's recording studios during the prolific 1960s. The roster of artists on these records include legendary Detroit soulsters Barbara Lewis, Deon Jackson, and The AdLibs. Other greats were The Soul Twins, Betty LaVette, and The Capitals. These legends all benefitted from Ollie's production skills.[5]

Sugar's dad and his Uncle Maxie joined their brother Ollie. The trio did gigs or concerts on weekends for various artists in nearby Ypsilanti and Ann Arbor. They promoted shows for artists such as Buddy Rich, Sarah Vaughan, Woodie Herman, Duke Ellington, Stan Getz, Lester Young, Ray Charles, John Coltrane, and Count Basie. In an effort to promote jazz, they featured The Dave Brubeck Quartet, Louis Armstrong, and Chet Baker.

Ollie was a stalwart in the Detroit music scene of the 1960s. People who worked with him praised him for his professional qualities that helped them maximize their talents. They also lauded him for being a stand-up person. Ollie died of a heart attack at age 58 in 1984, but his legacy lives on. His son Ira would ultimately go into the music business like his dad. Ira landed a job with Atlantic Records, engineering and working with such well-known artists as the

Rolling Stones, the Bee Gees, Whitney Houston, and Luther Vandross.

Even today, people dance to the music Ollie McLaughlin produced. Among the hit records he produced in the early and mid-1960s were: Del Shannon's 1961 #1 hit "Runaway" and "Hats Off to Larry," Barbara Lewis's "Baby I'm Yours" and "Make Me Your Baby," "Love Makes the World Go Round" by Deon Jackson, and "Cool Jerk" by the Capitols.[6] In 2018, Ollie was elected into the Michigan Rock and Roll Legends Hall of Fame.

Sugar's Uncle Maxie and his wife Venie ran a boarding house for students and guests. It was ideally located near the University of Michigan's campus. They hosted many black musicians and entertainers when they were in town. As a result, Sugar and his family came to know some of the personalities in the music and entertainment business. Locals included Martha Jean "The Queen" Steinberg, Dorothy and Donnie Simpson, and Berry Gordy. The Queen was a pioneering female disc jockey for Detroit's WJLB FM. She eventually became more well known for her focus on gospel and social commentary than R&B.

Simpson's record shop was especially popular during the booming music industry in Detroit. One of their sons, Donnie, who started out as a teen DJ for WJBL, would achieve fame for becoming America's first Video DJ for BETV. Gordy founded the Motown Record Corporation in 1960. The "Motown Sound" featured the artists Smokey Robinson, Mary Wells, the Supremes, Marvin Gaye, and the Temptations. Other greats included Jimmy Ruffin, the Contours, the Four Tops, Gladys Knight & the Pips, the Commodores, the Velvelettes, Martha and the Vandellas, Stevie Wonder, and the Jackson 5.

The stars of the TV show "Amos 'n Andy," actors Alvin Childress and Spencer Williams, were also guests at the McLaughlin house.[7] Another guest at Uncle Maxie's and Aunt Venie's boardinghouse was a pretty, light-complexioned young lady named Ruth Toomes, who had started working at the University of Michigan library. When Ruth's previous landlady discovered that she was black, she evicted Ruth, who then needed housing. She had met Ollie earlier in the marketplace. Surprisingly, he was moving out of the same house where he had lived since he was a teenager, when she was moving in. They began dating and were married in 1958.[8]

However, for young Sugar, the most unforgettable guests at the boarding house were the Harlem Globetrotters, who stopped by for a visit whenever they happened to be in the area for a game. As a result, Sugar got to meet such legendary players as Meadowlark Lemon, Freddie "Curly" Neal, Leon Hillard, Hallie Bryant, and Bob "Showboat" Hall.

His dad's side of the family provided plenty of music and entertainment in Sugar's formative years. But his mother brought the most music and fun into the McLaughlin household. Mary Ruth McLaughlin was the life of the party, funny, full of laughter, and of course, a lover of music! She kept the family atmosphere silly, loose, and fun, while dealing with the more serious task of raising a family in the midst of the Civil Rights Movement, Vietnam War protests, and the questioning of societal norms. Sugar's brother Bobbie says with enthusiasm of his first best friend and the main woman in his life, "She was just out of sight!"

But Sugar had a special bond with his mom. "I had a really, really close relationship with my mom, as the baby of the family. While she was here, I was a little Mama's Boy. She made sure that I was always taken care of and that I was doing all right. She knew I loved to play basketball. But I was a good student. I did my homework and made sure I got all my assignments done on time."

Bobbie Sr. decided to leave Ann Arbor for Grand Rapids, to be closer to his sister Georgia, after their other sister died. It might have been a bit traumatic for Sugar as an eight-year-old.

The move would mean leaving behind his friends and relatives in Ann Arbor and being labeled "The New Kid" in school. Further, he wouldn't be able to attend the University of Michigan Wolverines' football and basketball games with his dad, brother Bobbie, and uncles and cousins, unless they were willing to make the two-hour drive from Grand Rapids. Nonetheless, Melvin looked forward to more fun, laughter and adventure in Grand Rapids, with his loving mom beside him, along with his dad and siblings.

Plus, there was always basketball to rely on as a constant. Though a bit on the shy side, he could make new friends in Grand Rapids on the basketball court. All he had to do was follow Uncle Ollie's motto and be nice to others. Before long, he would become known as a Real Cool Scooby Doo by his peers. With a basketball in the grasp of his hands, Sugar joined his family in their move to Grand Rapids.

6

HOME COURT ADVANTAGE IN GRAND RAPIDS

> One of the things I've noticed—if you got a hoop in your driveway and your game is good, you make friends real fast.

— CALDWELL BANKER COMMERCIAL, HOOPS

The summer prior to the McLaughlins' move to Grand Rapids, a three-day uprising in the "Furniture City" began around 2 a.m. on Tuesday, July 25. It lasted until noon on July 27, 1967. Underlying causes of the uprising were the extreme poverty, joblessness, poor schooling, and growing segregation in Grand Rapids. The black community had grown frustrated and restless. An estimate of a thousand people, both black and white, participated in the riot with 44 injuries and over 320 arrests. The damage cost approximately $500,000—around $3.5 million when adjusted to inflation.[1]

Former Ottawa Hills star Fred Brown is one of Grand Rapids' greatest basketball players. He was one of the young athletes recruited to help calm the teens during that summer of civil unrest. He and Harold Morris, now a Grand Rapids pastor, once responded to looting at a supermarket on Jefferson Avenue SE. They were both shot by a state police trooper while getting out of the car. No one was charged.[2]

Prior to the uprising, during the 1950s and 1960s, the black population in Grand Rapids surged as people moved to the city looking for jobs. Historically around 1% in 1940, the black population increased to around 11% by 1970. Due to racial prejudices and policies, the vast majority of these blacks were relegated to live in the city's older south-side neighborhoods. These neighborhoods became known as "the blackbelt" of Grand Rapids.[3]

The uprising, along with the expansion of US 131 and construction of US I-96, doubly affected Grand Rapids' city landscape. Together, they hastened the exodus of whites out of the city. In 1962, US 131 was made into an elevated highway, providing a thoroughfare that connected the north-end suburbs with the south-end suburbs. The expansion of US 131 did not come without controversy. It forced more than a thousand families from their homes. Leveling dozens of historic buildings, it resulted in an S-shaped curve around the remaining structures. Three years later, on the city's north side, crews tore down warehouses, homes, and both commercial and government buildings to accommodate commuters traveling to work from the east and west suburbs on Interstate 96.[4]

Both US 131 and I-96 provided easy access for whites living in the city's outer limits and suburbs. They could travel to and from work in downtown Grand Rapids, while avoiding its black residents in the nearby south-side neighborhoods. The resulting white flight of the city's residents magnified the need to integrate Grand Rapids Public Schools. These integration policies would directly affect Sugar starting in the eighth grade, when he would be transferred to another school district.

About the time the McLaughlins were moving into Grand Rapids on the city's south side, many south-side whites were moving out. They had already fled or were in the process of fleeing to the suburbs or outer city limits in search of more homogeneous neighborhoods. But as an eight-year-old, Sugar wasn't concerned about the particular skin color his new neighbors would have in Grand Rapids. The only colors he was concerned were orange, black, and white—shooting an orange ball with black ribs into a white net—as well as the colors of the uniforms when he happened to be playing or watching a game.

Actually, his biggest worry was whether or not his new neighborhood would have a nearby basketball court to play on. Each night before climbing into bed, he got down on his knees on pray. He would ask his heavenly Father to provide a playground within walking distance of their new house in Grand Rapids.

After finding temporary housing in Grand Rapids, Sugar's prayers were answered! The family eventually settled into a house on Prince Street. Built in 1923, their new home featured lots of natural woodwork, four bedrooms, two baths, a finished basement, a two-stall garage, and a fenced-in yard.

But the best feature of their new house, as far as Sugar was concerned? It was located only a minute's walk away west from Franklin Park. Franklin Park is on the south side of Franklin Street, between Fuller Avenue and Benjamin Avenue, and north of Alexander Street. As soon as he beheld the full court basketball courts at the park, Sugar found his home away from home in Grand Rapids. When he wanted to escape from the bonds of life's worries and cares, he could just wander down the street. After crossing Fuller Avenue, he entered the promised land of Franklin Park. The playgrounds would be flowing with jump shots and the sweet sound of swooshes as basketballs entered and exited its chain nets.

Franklin Park was the hangout place for the top basketball players in the city. There Sugar first developed his reputation as an outstanding basketball player as a youth. Competing against older and stronger players at the park motivated him to elevate his game even further. After all, he didn't want to be left standing on the sidelines when it came to choosing sides for the full court 5 on 5 matches.

In the summer months, he often put in a full day at the park working on his game, even after dark. And throughout the year, he habitually got in his daily shots regardless of the ever-changing West Michigan weather. In the winter he shoveled the snow from the courts. In the spring and summer months he swept off any leftover puddles from the rain. In the fall, he removed any excess leaves, branches, and twigs that had fallen from the trees.

If heaven was a playground, then Franklin Park was for Sugar the closest place on earth to paradise. Jacob had a vision of angels climbing up and down a ladder reaching to heaven at Bethel. When he awakened after that vision, he said, "Surely the Lord is in this place!" (see Genesis 28:16.) Similarly, Franklin Park became a sacred place where Sugar could sense the joy of God's presence, while playing basketball. Incidentally, when Dr. James Naismith first invented the game of basketball, players also climbed up and down a ladder to retrieve shots from peach baskets hung ten feet above the floor.

In 1969, Franklin Park was renamed Martin Luther King, Jr. Park in honor of the slain civil rights leader, after he was assassinated in 1968. The park is commonly referred to as simply King Park by local residents, though some patrons, especially those who were around before the name change, still refer to the playground by its original name of Franklin Park.

When he got older, Sugar would help carry out the vision of the park's namesake by refusing to judge the worth of basketball players based upon their skin color. Only playing skills mattered, when he welcomed a couple of white players at the park.

As eighth graders, Joe LaVoie and Garde Thompson rode their bikes to King Park for the first time. As LaVoie recalls, "We got some strange looks, as to what we were doing there, but then Sugar spoke up. 'They're running with me!' We ended up winning the rest of the games that day. And ever since, we felt at home, being endorsed by the best player in the park."

Thompson adds, "Melvin said, 'Those boys are with me. They can play.' The next thing you know other white kids would start showing up at the Park to play. Kids like Chris Mendez, Joe Baumgartner, Jimmy Boylen. All because Mel said it was okay. He ran the show. He was like the Godfather of King Park." LaVoie would become the all-time leading assist maker for Catholic Central High School ('83); Garde Thompson would star for East Grand Rapids High School ('83) and the University of Michigan ('87).

Looking back, I might have joined Garde and Joe that summer in their bicycle rides to King Park. Garde was a grade behind me and lived a few blocks away. His dad, the former varsity basketball coach at East, used to open up our Breton Downs Elementary School's gym on Saturday mornings in the winter for us to play. I didn't know Joe at the time, but I knew several of his Catholic Central teammates from attending Aquinas College's basketball camp. We would have certainly intertwined in the basketball circles of suburban East Grand Rapids.

However, that summer, I was out of state for a family work-vacation. I recall protesting to my mom about having to miss playing basketball all that time. "Can't I stay with one of my friends?" I pleaded. "Please, please!" After all, I was about to enter high school. Plus, East Grand Rapids had just gotten a new basketball coach. I wanted to impress him during the open gym sessions at our high school.

If my parents had given in to my protests, I might have gotten to know Sugar earlier. I may have been one of the white players selected with Garde and Joe to join his team at King Park. Most certainly, Sugar would have inspired me to be a better basketball player. With his encouragement and by playing against the stiffer competition at King Park, I probably wouldn't have been as shaky in the throes of competition in actual games. Instead, I would have been as confident on the court as I was on my parent's driveway, swishing outside jumpers with ease. I may have even lived up to one of my nicknames in Junior High, "Saccharine," as a substitute for "Sugar." My so-called basketball career might have turned out quite differently than it did.

At the same time, there were other opportunities for me to have played at King Park, if I wanted to. But I had other courts to play on, and frequented them as often as possible. But that one summer proved pivotal in my basketball journey.

Interestingly, our lives turn on simple decisions or events. Had I met Sugar earlier, who knows what might have happened, and the heights my basketball career might have attained? But God had other plans for me and my basketball aspirations.

Boylen, Thompson's teammate at East Grand Rapids ('83), went on to play for the University of Maine ('87). After his playing days were over, he coached several Division I and NBA teams, including as head coach of the Chicago Bulls. He groomed his playing skills at the Park.

 I lived at King Park, but I knew it as Franklin Park. That's where I learned how to play. I have taken my kids there. They have shot on those rims. I remember playing guys in their work clothes, because they just got out of their shift at the factory. And I remember playing under the lights and guys betting on us while we were playing. I was the only white guy in the park a few times.

The first time I was there I was the last guy picked. I played one game and then I was the first guy picked.

King Park has been featured in Chris Ballard's *Hoops Nation: A Guide to America's Best Pickup Basketball,* Jamaal Al-Din's *Hoops 227 blog* and web site, as well as in a book by *Sports Illustrated* writer Alexander Wolff on the nation's top basketball playgrounds. When Ballard wrote his book, he reported that the backboards at King Park all said, "Play fair, stay cool—No trash talk or profanity." But players paid about as much attention to this as a three-second call on the playground. From April through August, the best players in the city would make it a nightly rendezvous to compete from roughly 6:30-9:00 p.m.[5]

Al-Din grew up in Mountain Home, Idaho, and used to visit his relatives in Grand Rapids during the summer months. He says, "King Park, for me, was always a chance to get better. Going back to Grand Rapids was interesting, because I knew how to shoot, but in the park, you had to add more to your game in terms of creativity."

Many other players developed their games at Franklin Park. They include Grand Rapids' area legends Michael "Pops" Sims, Steven "Preacher" Lee, and Roosevelt "Rose Show" Pritchett. Anthony Welch, Andre Harris, Loy Vaught, Mike Davenport, and Justin Jennings also improved their shots at the legendary playground. Others include Thomas Kelly, Jamie Cole, Marte Smith, Geno Carlisle, Lacy Jones, Michael Spicer, Anthony Soule, Eric Taylor, Thomas Kilgore, Matt Stewart, Steve Schefler, and Sugar's nephew, Eric McLaughlin.

Sugar became known as the best player in the area. But he would have to prove over and over that he was "the man" and still King of King Park. As he commented prior to the 11th annual TA-WA-SI All-Star game in 1983, "In the playgrounds, everybody can show their best moves, best dribble, and best shot. A lot of players come to the park every day and test you. They know you have a big name (in high school), and they want to see if you are really that good. You play them because you have pride."[6]

Sugar also became a frequent figure on the court of Kelloggsville Middle School while growing up. Bobbie Sr., with his experience working in the cleaning business in Ann Arbor, found a job as a cleaner in Grand Rapids. He was also able to supplement his income by cleaning on weekends at Kelloggsville Middle School, located in the southwest side of Grand Rapids. As a result, Sugar was able to work on his game in a regular gym and didn't have to worry about any changes in the outdoor weather. The only thing he did have to concern himself with was to be sure to help his dad out before he got his shots in. Occasionally, his dad would join him. Even though he was more of a baseball player, having been an outfielder in the Negro League, Bobbie McLaughlin Sr. had a nice little hook shot that he enjoyed showing off to his younger son.

Little did Sugar know that he was practicing in the same gym where one of his future mentors had once played. Don "The Animal" Edwards went on to star for the Kelloggsville High School Rockets in the early 1960s. After graduation he had a Hall of Fame career at Central Michigan (1962-1966) and played for the Grand Rapids Tackers (1969-1973). Though only 6 feet tall and 180 pounds, Edwards was nicknamed The Animal for his aggressive style of play. He was also known for his shooting touch. In addition to playing for the Tackers, Edwards taught physical education at Grand Rapids Creston for over 35 years. He also taught at Grand Rapids Community College, and served as a Division I football and basketball referee.[7] In 2005, Edwards died of cancer at age 61.

When Sugar came to Creston, Edwards taught him to use the backboard effectively. They also competed in shooting matches between classes. The Animal became a charter member of CMU's Athletic Hall of Fame in 1984. Sugar would join him there in 1993. In 2005, shortly after Edward's death, he and Edwards were inducted at the same time into the Grand Rapids Sports Hall of Fame. Sugar was particularly moved while giving a speech at the ceremony, as he recalled Edwards' impact on his life. He wished he could have been there to celebrate their achievements together. All of Sugar's involvement in young lives stems from mentors like Edwards. He has never forgotten.

Another court Sugar frequented growing up was Campau Park. Campau Park is located at 50 Antoine Street South West, south of Franklin Street and west of Division Avenue. Division serves as the east-west dividing line of the city. Before blacks in Grand Rapids began to move near Franklin Park in the 1960s, Campau Park was one of their main hangouts in the 1940s and 1950s. Sugar's aunt lived nearby. Conveniently, New Hope Baptist Church (130 Delaware Street SW), the McLaughlin family's home church, was a few blocks from the park.

At Campau, Sugar encountered Ernie Johnson, the park's recreational leader. The 6'8" Johnson had led Ottawa Hills High School to back-to-back championships in 1968-1969. Johnson would go on to play for the University of Michigan (1971-1973), averaging 9.9 points and 7.4 rebounds per game where he started 37 of 38 games his junior and senior years, and proceeded to play a couple of years for the Tackers (1973-1975). He went on to become a leader and long-time educator in the Grand Rapids Public School District.[8] He also served seven years as head basketball coach at Union and one season as coach at Ottawa Hills. At the park, Johnson offered advice and encouragement to younger players, such as Sugar, while serving as a role model. When he got older, Sugar teamed up with Johnson in an annual TA-WA-SI game. Johnson died February 15, 2018 at age 67, but his son Arian remains close friends with Sugar.

Occasionally, for a change of scenery and to challenge different players, Sugar journeyed up to the courts at Sigsbee Park. Located between 431-499 Benjamin Avenue SE, the park is about .6 miles north of King Park and about half a mile northeast of the Baxter Community Center in the Eastown Neighborhood of Grand Rapids. Michael Brown recalls,

 Besides having absolutely phenomenal ability, Sugar put in the work. From high school going on into college, I worked with him at Sigsbee Park. After cleaning up, all we did was play. He had solo drills which were so intense and incredibly difficult. He would spin three times to the left (180 degrees) then shoot what would be a three-pointer. He would then immediately reverse direction and repeat the shot. After he left, I would simply try to spin that fast without a ball and would be dizzy. It always looked so easy for him in the games, but I witnessed him put in that work.

The Baxter Community Center can also claim, "Sugar played here." The Center where Sugar picked up his nickname in elementary school still exists. Located on 935 Baxter Street SE, the Center resulted from a vision first cast in the late 1960s. Members of the Eastern Avenue Christian Reformed Church sought to address sociological issues in tangible ways. With neighbors, they tackled civil strife, urban decay, and pervasive racial inequality. Originally housed above Bierline Bakery on Eastern Avenue, in 1969, the Center moved to the former site of Baxter Christian School. Providentially, the school had recently closed at the end of the 1968-1969 school year.

For its first official executive director, the board chose Herschel Turner. Turner had been a star basketball player at the University of Nebraska. He then played for the Chicago Majors, Pittsburgh Pipers, Harlem Globetrotters and the Grand Rapids Tackers. Turner was also a gifted artist and a respected leader in the Grand Rapids community. Through his passion and leadership, young people began to flock to the programs created for them. In the summer, hundreds of kids came each day to play basketball, receive a free meal and spend their days in a safe and welcoming environment.[9]

Joining Turner on Baxter's staff was his Tackers' teammate, George Knighton, the mentor who would nickname Sugar. Sugar frequented the Baxter Community Center after school and would play for Alexander Elementary School there. In high school, he demonstrated his skills in the summer Baxter Community basketball tournament, outshining the area's other prep stars. The Baxter Community Center continues to be a safe haven for neighborhood children. They head there for after school activities, such as playing basketball, especially for those who cannot afford a gym membership. Again, the seeds of Sugar's community compassion were sown by loving and generous members of Grand Rapids.

Still another court where Sugar left his mark was at the Paul I. Phillips Recreation Center. The gym at 726 Madison Ave SE was formerly owned and operated by the Grand Rapids Christian Schools. It had been the home court for Grand Rapids Christian High School. Plus, Calvin College played most of their home games there before the 1965 construction of Knollcrest Fieldhouse. After using the gymnasium for its park and recreation programs since 1974, the city officially acquired the gym in the late 1970s. In 1983, the gymnasium was named Paul I. Phillips Recreation Center after a former director of the Grand Rapids Urban League. Phillips had set a state record in track at Central High School (class of '32). During the turbulent civil rights struggles of the 1950s and 1960s, he led the Urban League Chapter in Grand Rapids, as a calm and strong force

against racial discrimination. He was the first African American
to hold an elected office in Grand Rapids.[10]

At Paul I. Phillips, Sugar got to know another former Grand
Rapids Tacker, 6'4" Delton Heard, who played for the team
from 1962-1967. William Brashler, who grew up watching the
Tackers in the 1960s, describes Heard:

 Delton Heard impressed us the most. A barrel-
chested, knock-kneed, droopy-eyed, ball-handling
magician, Heard once came on to the court with
his shorts on backwards. Heard's Globetrotter-like
repertoire included a one-on-three fast break in
which he would bank the ball off the backboard
back to himself and stuff the rebound. I think the
play was illegal, but we were amazed by it.[11]

When Heard hung up his basketball shoes, he served as a
director of Activities at the Youth Commonwealth-Seidman
Youth Center. In 1974, he joined the Grand Rapids Recreation
Department as a Recreation Supervisor for the area parks and
managed the Paul I. Phillips Gym. There, he would excel in
providing guidance, direction, and basketball tips to many
Grand Rapids area youth. At the same time, he enforced the
necessary discipline. Heard was called home to rest on March
31, 2003 at age 61 from leukemia.[12]

Phillips has been the site for recreation basketball leagues
over the years, including Midnight Basketball Games in the
1990s. Those games were part of a nationwide initiative to curb
inner-city crime in the United States. Between the prime crime
hours of 10 p.m. and 2 a.m., young people from ages 14-25,
mostly men of color, could play basketball. They could also
attend programs that offered helpful skills for everyday life. On
occasion, Philips has served as the host of the annual TA-WA-SI
All-Star Game, a Grand Rapids scholarship organization for

black youth. (TaWaSi is a Native American name meaning Friend and Helper.) Begun in 1973 by Herman Green Jr. and Granville Brown, the Games featured some of the top players in the area on an annual basis through 2005.[13]

In the 1979 TA-WA-SI All-Star Game, a jam-packed crowd at Philips saw Magic Johnson and Gregory Kelser play. The dynamic duo was fresh off winning the National Championship for Michigan State over Larry's Bird's Indiana State Sycamores. Besides Magic, Special K, and Sugar, other legends gracing Philips with their presence include George "The Iceman" Gervin and Isiah Thomas.[14] Similar to King Park, most all the star players out of Grand Rapids, at one time or another, have laced up their shoes in this historic gym.

Ricky Hampton Senior, a former sports writer for *Booth* Newspapers, covering the Lions and the Pistons, recalls his first encounter watching Sugar play at Philips a few years ago. Knowing that Hampton would be visiting Grand Rapids, Dave Ginsberg advised him, "Look for a guy they call Sugar." Hampton asked, "Who's Sugar?" Ginsberg's eyes twinkled. "You'll find out!"

Sure enough, Hampton stopped by the historic gym for a work out. He says,

 I'm watching the game and see this older guy shooting and making baskets from all over the place. He isn't missing. He might have made about 29 out of 32 of his shots and they were all from 35 feet or more. I'm thinking, that old guy is having one lucky day. I commented to the others watching the game with me, "Who is that guy?" They all laughed, saying, "That's Sugar!" I had to call Gins afterward and tell him "I found Sugar! Now I know what you mean!" I'll never forget that. It was the greatest shooting display

I'd ever seen in all my years of covering basketball.

Sugar has burned the nets in a variety of courts in the Grand Rapids area over the years. These include the gyms where he played in middle and high school, as well as in recreational and pro-am leagues. And who can count the places where he's swished shots for his Sugar Mel All-Star Teams, doing fundraising events, putting on clinics, and playing pick-up games?

However, one gym where Sugar hardly got a chance to break a sweat was my former gym at East Grand Rapids (EGR) High School. East Grand Rapids is an enclave just east of the city limits, consisting of mostly middle- to upper-middle-class white people. During Sugar's time, the Creston Polar Bears belonged to the City League. The EGR Pioneers were members of the OK-Red Conference along with some of the bigger suburban schools in the area. Consequently, Creston and "The Easties" didn't play each other in the regular season. But this wasn't the only reason Sugar failed to swish a lot of shots in the Pioneers' home gymnasium.

Sugar had introduced some of the EGR players to inner-city ball at King Park. One player, Garde Thompson, often invited him to come play at our high school's home court. Sugar accepted his offer and got some of the top players in the city to join him. Presumably, one of the EGR residents saw all these young black men outside of the high school and reported them to the local police. As Sugar explains,

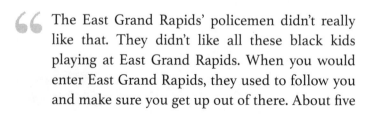 The East Grand Rapids' policemen didn't really like that. They didn't like all these black kids playing at East Grand Rapids. When you would enter East Grand Rapids, they used to follow you and make sure you get up out of there. About five

or six of us inner-city boys were in the gym. We were playing with the East Grand Rapids' players, because they wanted to go against the top competition.

Soon after they started playing, EGR's football coach at that time, George Barcheski (aka "Bar"), stormed into the gym. Sugar goes on to say,

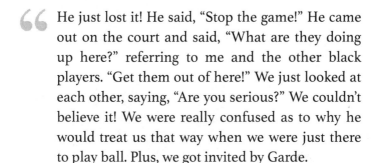 He just lost it! He said, "Stop the game!" He came out on the court and said, "What are they doing up here?" referring to me and the other black players. "Get them out of here!" We just looked at each other, saying, "Are you serious?" We couldn't believe it! We were really confused as to why he would treat us that way when we were just there to play ball. Plus, we got invited by Garde.

Sugar will never forget that incident. Although, he does concede that Bar may have been having a bad day or else feeling pressure from the neighbors and the police for letting these inner-city boys play in EGR's gym. He also admires the way Bar embraced Jimmy Gerken, a mentally-challenged young man in the community. Bar made Jimmy an integral part of his football program. Barcheski, a Hall of Fame coach and winner of five state titles, died in 2008 at the age of 82. In spite of this encounter, Sugar graciously acknowledges, "He was a good coach!"

Thompson, whose dad, Chuck, was a long-time assistant coach for Barcheski, has a different spin on the incident. "You know Bar. It was the beginning of football season. And he was all about football, not basketball. Nothing better get in the way of football! As far as he was concerned, the gym wasn't open for basketball anymore."

In this new millennium, Grand Rapids had added even more choices where Sugar could possibly play basketball. In nearby Byron Center, the Courthouse Athletic Center of Grand Rapids is a private facility. Designed specifically for basketball, volleyball, and fitness, it opened in 2000. The MVP Sports Complex opened in March, 2005 on Burton Street SE, designed after the theme of the Orlando Magic. Additional MVP clubs were added to the Grand Rapids area later. The David D. Hunting YMCA in downtown Grand Rapids, also built in 2005, has beautiful courts that can fill up pretty fast by the locals. The Ray & Joan Kroc Corps Community Center, 2500 South Division Ave., opened in 2010 featuring some of the top indoor and outdoor courts in the area.

Today, more often than not you can catch Sugar playing at the MVP Sportsplex after work and on weekends. But ask him which court, of all the choices in the Grand Rapids area, is his main home court. He'll say without hesitation, "King Park!"

Just as the park's namesake had a dream, so Sugar pursued his hoop dreams on the court nearest his boyhood home on Prince Street. Countless hours in pursuit of that dream at King Park earned him the "King of basketball" in Grand Rapids, and one of the greatest long-range shooters in the history of the game. The park's original name of Franklin also fits his unique style of play. Benjamin Franklin is famous for his innovations and inventions. Like Franklin, Sugar is a paradigm pioneer. He may not have been welcomed in the East Grand Rapids' Pioneers home gymnasium, but he paved a new way to play the game of basketball, consistently launching shots from an unprecedented long range.

A Patron Saint is believed to give special help to a particular place, activity, person, or type of object. Sugar might be considered the patron saint of King Park. Swing by some Saturday morning. Even now, you'll find him at the park, training kids and helping them take their best shot.

7

SWEET SHOT

> God will give you a lot of things in life, but he's not going to give you your jump shot. Only hard work will do that.
>
> — Ray Allen, NBA Champion

I n 1968, Sugar's family couldn't afford to send him to a basketball camp, like he wanted. If they had, he might have developed a more orthodox shooting form. Instead, his technique of shooting a basketball is truly unique. Much like the apostle Paul's vision of heaven, it defies description. Unfortunately, there's little actual footage of Sugar's unconventional shooting style available. Those who witnessed him shoot have likened his shot to a slingshot, a shot put, an overhand boomerang, a tomahawk, a bomb hitting its target, a radar, a guided missile, and a lasso.

Basketball shooting experts advise younger players to begin shooting baskets using a smaller ball at a goal of lower height. This instills a muscle memory of proper shooting form as they mature. For while practice can lead to perfection, it can also lead to permanence, and a poor shooting habit can be difficult to break. Players who lack strength tend to chuck a standard-sized ball at a 10-foot goal and thus end up being to the left or the right of their intended target.

In contrast, players with the correct form when shooting a basketball usually end up being on target. Consequently, when their shot is off, they can readily adjust by adding or subtracting to their shot's length. As Tim Ferris writes, "If you can control the flight of the ball to the point where you don't miss left or right, it's only a matter of time before misses that are short or long correct themselves. Short or long misses are easy to correct. Misses left and right mean that something is wrong with your shot form."[1]

Sugar, however, had developed his form shooting a regular ball into a standard ten-foot-high goal, again and again. On top of that, when he first started playing, most of the players he faced were older, taller and stronger. He learned to shoot the basketball from further distances, in spite of how unorthodox his shot may have been. As he explains his strategy, "I was so little, so I taught myself to shoot from places where people didn't think I was going to. When I started making those shots and they ran out to guard me, I would drive right past them."

At first Sugar relied on a chest shot, pushing the ball from his chest in order to generate enough strength to reach the ten-foot basketball goal. But before long, he says, "I learned to shoot behind my head, because players would come after me to block my shot. I had to bring the ball back farther in order to get my shot off."

Todd Stacey refers to himself as "being cursed" to have been assigned to guard Sugar while playing for West Middle School and Union High School.

 I was noted as a pretty doggone good defender. But Melvin could pull up from just anywhere, once he made it to the hash mark. His shot wasn't a classic form. He had this unique thing, where he would take the ball from the side to the center of his head, and just let it fly with his right hand. He would touch the ball slightly with his left hand, but it was pretty much a one-handed shot. It was hard to stop him, because he would just throw it up from anywhere. He's barely six foot and I think I might have nicked his shot once the whole time I guarded him. He had that style for as long as I guarded him, from middle school through high school.

Jimmy Boylen guarded Sugar while playing at King Park. He comments,

> I could usually stop people by forcing them to go to their weak-hand side, but Sugar could shoot going both ways the same. I'm trying to chase him around, and get the ball from him, and prevent him from shooting. But with his dribble move, he would end up going either way. It's unusual for a scorer to have the ability to shoot from as far out as he did from both sides. Who's going to stop that? He would pull up for his shot using both hands. There's not a shot blocker around that could prevent him from getting his shots off, which is pretty special.

Scott McNeal witnessed Sugar play live and close enough to touch him in his Gus Macker 3 on 3 Tournaments. He adds,

> His ability to shoot was just crazy in the tournament. If you stood behind him and

watched him shoot within a couple of feet, it was pretty interesting how his shot would just take off. Within a ten-foot circle, you could double-, triple-, even quadruple-team him and somehow, he could get his shot off. He had a crossover, behind the back thing. But he could shoot it so crazy-fast, and he'd shoot it behind his head, so that nobody could block it. It was amazing!

Johnny Brann has been a Sugar fan since he first saw him play in high school. Brann insists that Mel was a better shooter than even Steph Curry!

> It's easy for me to say Sugar was a better shooter than Curry, based on the fact that I know him so well and I love him as a person. Plus, he's a legend from Grand Rapids. Curry's amazing, but honestly, Sugar was a better shooter, in my opinion, because he could create his own shot. You could have your hand right in his face. It didn't matter. He just shot over you.

Over the years, people have tried to get him to change his form. Some wanted him to straighten out his shooting arm to form a more conventional backwards "L". Others encouraged him to release the ball from above his head rather than behind it. However, Sugar's muscle memory has been permanently ingrained in him given long hours of practice on the basketball court. Besides, his shot is so accurate that there has been little incentive for him or others to change his signature form.

Before an eighth-grade basketball practice at East Grand Rapids Junior High's gym, some teammates and I started to shoot around. We tried shooting from way beyond our normal range, attempting to imitate Sugar's shooting style. We yelled

"Sugar!" at the same time, hoping to get similar results as him. Our coach, Mark Howard, after beholding our sorry attempts of trying "to be like Sugar," immediately curtailed our shooting exhibition. Though laughing at our antics, he shouted at us, "Shoot the ball the way you're supposed to! There's only one Sugar and you're not him!"

Sugar also has unusually large hands for his size, with wide palms and extraordinary long fingers. Some have compared his hand size to legendary players Julius "Dr. J" Irving and Connie Hawkins, both known for their ability to palm the basketball and for outstanding ball control. On the one hand, having big hands may be an advantage for Sugar, giving him a unique grip of the ball when it comes to dribbling and shooting.

On the other hand, some have theorized that big hands lead to bad shooting. They reason that shooting a basketball is usually centered in a fingertip-and-wrist motion, without involving the palm. However, players with larger hands tend to have too much palm involved in their shot. As a result, there isn't space between their palm and the ball, which can more easily throw off their shot. A player with unusually big hands shooting a basketball can be compared to someone with average-sized hands shooting a softball or tennis ball. They can end up shot-putting their shots with very little motion in the elbow/wrist area, rather than shooting a basketball by snapping their wrist. This explains why players with larger hands, like Wilt Chamberlain and Shaquille O'Neal, are characteristically poor free throw shooters.

However, Sugar has worked so hard on his game, and shot so many shots, that he's overcome any possible impediment the size of his hands may cause. In spite of his less-than-textbook shooting form, he is able to finish his shots with all the mechanics in their proper place. His head coach at Central Michigan University, Dick Parfitt, had a reputation for being an old school coach given his emphasis on the fundamentals of the game. He once said, "Melvin has what you'd call a picture shot. When he finishes, everything (hand, wrist, fingers) is going towards the basket. It's so fundamentally sound you couldn't teach it any better."[2]

Even if you happen to watch Sugar play on film, it's nearly impossible to depict what it was like to witness him shoot in person. Footage couldn't capture his jaw-dropping performances. Not only could he score while facing heavy opposition in indoor games, outdoors he could score while facing unusually windy conditions. Scott McNeal says, "The thing about seeing him play outdoors is that he's making these shots in the wind. People watching wonder how he is able to do this? His shots are going in from everywhere he happens to shoot them. Everyone else's shots are going everywhere but in the basket."

Jamaal Al-Adin grew up watching Sugar play when visiting relatives in Grand Rapids. He reasons that film couldn't depict just how wild it was to see him shoot. Seeing him play in the gym was one thing. It was another to see him play outside in the Gus Macker Tournament or at the Park. His big-time shooting was simply amazing. Al-Adin describes this in his *Hoops 227* blog. "Put it this way, with a 45-mph wind blowing in 8 different directions Sugar Mel could shoot the lights out from 3-point range."[3]

Garde Thompson was an exceptional outside shooter for East Grand Rapids High School and then the University of Michigan. He once had nine three-pointers to lead the Wolverines over David Robinson's Midshipman of the Navy in the first round of the 1987 NCAA tournament. Even he says, "I would never want to take Sugar on in a game of H-O-R-S-E, because I can't shoot from that far back. I can't physically even throw it that far. It's astounding what he can do. I can take him to the basket because of my jumping ability. It was always fun when we played each other because we had such contrasting styles of play."

Today, Sugar continues to launch shots from far out using the same signature shooting style he developed as a little kid. His iconic shooting silhouette is emblazoned on the back of the Sugar Mel's camp T-shirts. The next generation of players can behold his form. But as far as coaching purists are concerned, such as my eighth-grade basketball coach, not necessarily to imitate!

8

A PLAYGROUND LEGEND

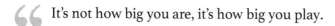

❝❝ It's not how big you are, it's how big you play.

— Unknown

A gifted all-around athlete, Sugar also played football in elementary school. Even in 1968, size and speed allowed him to excel in Rocket football. However, as one of the smallest players, he heeded his dad's advice and hung up his cleats before he got seriously hurt. Sugar also shined on the baseball field.

He looked up to his older brother Bobbie, a promising prospect in the Double-A Minor League. Bobbie played for the Grand Rapids Sullivans, a semi-pro baseball team and one of the top amateur teams in the country, before his knees blew out.

Thankfully, Sugar's devotion to basketball took precedence over any other sport. He was a student of the game and of those who excelled at it. As he describes,

I got to be better than others, because I worked so diligently on my game. I was always in the park. I was always practicing and doing drills that I had learned from basketball camps and watching other legends that were ahead of me. I emulated a lot of pros and took different aspects from their games, then worked on incorporating them into mine.

Among the star professional players Sugar would seek to emulate on the court were Julius "Dr. J." Irving, George "Iceman" Gervin, "Pistol" Pete Maravich, and Earl "The Pearl" Monroe. In addition, Grand Rapids had its own share of local and national star players that he watched live and in person, then copied their moves.

Bobbie realized just how much his younger brother lived and breathed the game of basketball. Occasionally, he treated Melvin to the Grand Rapids' Tackers games at Godwin Heights High School or the downtown Civic Center. The semi-pro Tackers played their home games to sellout crowds from 1961 to 1974, drawing over 3,000 fans per game. Not only did Sugar watch some of their games, he got to know some of the Tackers personally at local parks and gyms. They invested in him, and offered him their tips and encouragement.

Indeed, the Tackers were more than a stadium-filling team. They embraced the community, and the community embraced them. I remember scoring my first official points as a basketball player before a Grand Rapids Tackers' crowd. In fourth grade, I made two outside shots at Godwin Heights High School. During half-time at a Tackers' game, our team at Hope Lutheran Church played an exhibition game against Martin Luther School. As we headed to the locker room, the waiting Tackers greeted us with their words of encouragement. "Good game!" "Nice shooting out there, hot shot!" "Way to go, champ!"

Then they took the floor to get ready for the second half of their game.

Given his young age, size and height, Sugar didn't appear to have much to offer when choosing sides for teams before the pick-up games on the playgrounds. But when finally given a chance, he made the most of the opportunity. As soon as he got into a game, he started taking and making shots at unexpectedly long distances. So much so that everyone simply stared in amazement and disbelief.

Playing before the advent of the 3-point rule made his shooting range even more astonishing. Back then, regardless of how close or far you were shooting from, every basket counted two points. Consequently, players were often discouraged from taking what were considered lower percentage shots from the outside by their coaches. Instead, they were encouraged to work the ball inside for higher percentage shots.

At first, when his teammates saw him eyeing the basket and about to shoot, they shouted, "Don't shoot it!" "You're too far away from the basket!" "Work it in for a better shot!" Then they noticed how consistently he made his shots. Their warnings of dissuasion changed into expressions of encouragement. Soon, instead of overlooking him on the court, his teammates began to look for Sugar to receive their pass, shouting, "Shoot it!" More often than not, Sugar responded by pulling up for a long-range jump shot, with an automatic *swoosh* of the chain nets.

It wasn't just his teammates and opponents on the court that took notice of his phenomenal shooting skills. Those on the sidelines started to marvel at the little kid with the big-time shot. As a result, they added their voices to the chorus of affirmations from his teammates on the court, encouraging him after each basket. "Do it again! Do it again!" they screamed for the rest of the game. After Sugar led his team to a victory, they cheered, "Next!" Everyone waited for him to take on another team of hapless victims on the sidelines. Once again, he would lead his team to hold court with his phenomenal range and playing skills. Afterward, his fans would respond by crying out their familiar refrain to the next team in waiting, "Next!"

After her encounter with Jesus at the well in Sychar, the Samaritan woman was quick to spread the news of meeting the promised Messiah. Through this many believed in Him. Similarly, many witnessed firsthand the God Thing in Sugar's playing ability on the basketball court. They couldn't possibly keep what they had seen to themselves. They began to tell others. Word spread from the playgrounds throughout the various neighborhoods in Grand Rapids. "There's a little kid who can sling jump shots from all over the basketball court. And invariably, he makes them over and over again."

Eventually, rumors of Sugar's astounding performances on the basketball court began to spread through the grapevines of Grand Rapids and into his brother Bobbie's ears. Some neighbors began asking him, "Have you seen your brother play?" and "Who taught him how to shoot like that?"

After hearing so much about his little brother's game, Bobbie wanted to see for himself how his little brother stacked up against some competition. He challenged a friend, who also had a younger brother, to a game of two-on-two. The loser had to treat the winning team to a couple of soda pops. His friend's little brother had the advantage of being older, bigger, and more physical than Sugar. When their two-on-two battle began, he tried to intimidate Sugar by roughing him up a bit. Sugar just shot further and further away from the basket. By now, he had become accustomed to shooting from long distances in order to score against older, taller, and stronger opponents. He wasn't fazed a bit.

As this duel clearly demonstrated, he had learned how to overcome any disadvantages he may have had due to his size. Not only did Bobbie and Sugar win the game and the sodas,

Bobbie witnessed for the first time his brother's superior shooting and playing skills. What he had heard from others, he had now seen personally. Ever since, he has been Sugar's number one fan, supporter, and promoter of his basketball aspirations. He already knew that God had given his little brother a special love for basketball, after that dramatic chase of a runaway ball at age four. But now Bobbie recognized more than Sugar's devotion to the game. God had gifted him with an almost supernatural ability to play the very game he loved. Consequently, Bobbie began to take Sugar with him on various runs in the city. They earned more free sodas in the process.

Bobbie wasn't the only one to recognize his baby brother's outstanding basketball skills. While suiting up for Alexander Elementary School at the Baxter Community Center, this skinny kid stood out from all the rest of the players. Sugar would lead his team to back-to-back league championships in fifth and sixth grades.

Sugar's superior gifts on the court would become both solace and sanctuary, in one of the hardest losses of his life.

9

FINDING A REFUGE IN BASKETBALL

❝ Basketball is my refuge, my sanctuary. I go back to being a kid on the playground. When I get here, it's all good.

— KOBE BRYANT

I n fifth grade, at the tender age of eleven, Sugar experienced a major loss in his life. His mom died from breast cancer at the age of forty-four. Her death left a vacuum in the McLaughlin house. Without her leavening influence of joy and laughter, the atmosphere of a home once filled with joyous love songs was transformed into a house of blues.

Bobbie explains, "We had always lived with anticipation, music and family and food and hope. My mom was so central to that. Mom and I were really close." Even now, his throat closes and he squeezes words past the tears. "She wasn't just my mom. She was my best friend. But she also had a special bond with Melvin as her youngest son. Moms are like that!"

Breast cancer took its toll. Mary Ruth McLaughlin beckoned her firstborn son closer to her bedside. She had a final request concerning her youngest child. Her voice was weak but determined. "Junior, I'm giving you the responsibility to make sure Melvin turns out right. Make sure he stays out of trouble and gets an education."

Bobbie responded to his mom's request with a solemn oath, "Yes, Momma!" Ever since, he has felt obligated to make sure his brother would become the person his mom would be proud of. Though he realized a tough road awaited them, he was determined to keep his promise. During her illness, he was in and out of home, but had his own apartment and friends he played baseball with. Everything changed with the mantle from his mother. Her death left his dad alone with Mel, and before long, with the nieces and nephews.

In his early twenties, Bobbie stepped in physically as well as financially to help, and reclaimed his old room to help his dad. He says,

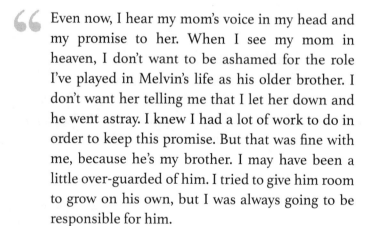

> Even now, I hear my mom's voice in my head and my promise to her. When I see my mom in heaven, I don't want to be ashamed for the role I've played in Melvin's life as his older brother. I don't want her telling me that I let her down and he went astray. I knew I had a lot of work to do in order to keep this promise. But that was fine with me, because he's my brother. I may have been a little over-guarded of him. I tried to give him room to grow on his own, but I was always going to be responsible for him.

Their mom's death was very difficult for the entire family, and particularly for Sugar as a preteen. As he reflects, "I was so young, and was so close to her. It was lonely. I had to mature quickly after she passed away." To add even further to the McLaughlins' house of mourning, their oldest sibling, Patricia, died of a drug overdose around a year later at 26, leaving behind six children: Renee, Tami, Dobbie, Nicky, Sandford, and James. According to Bobbie, she couldn't continue after the death of their mom. She simply didn't want to live anymore.

In the span of a little over a year, their father lost his beloved wife and firstborn daughter. He tried his best to cope. Adding to the emotional weight after Pat's death, he took in three of her youngest children. This added even more to his burden as the main breadwinner and disciplinarian of the family. Understandably, he became a lot more serious and much less fun to be around. Sugar remembers, "He was strict! He was always making sure that everything was equipped and everyone was doing what they were supposed to be doing."

In looking back at this difficult time in their lives, the family recognizes just how challenging it must have been for their dad. Bobbie empathizes,

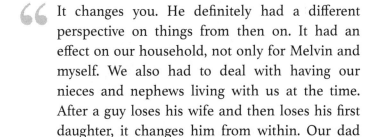

> It changes you. He definitely had a different perspective on things from then on. It had an effect on our household, not only for Melvin and myself. We also had to deal with having our nieces and nephews living with us at the time. After a guy loses his wife and then loses his first daughter, it changes him from within. Our dad had a different perspective when it came to raising the kids still in the house.

Sugar responded by finding refuge on the basketball court. "Sports were my solace. My main thing was to play ball. I was always out at the parks. That was my outlet for staying away from all the ruckus and the noise at home." In addition, he put his nephews and nieces to work, getting them to retrieve his shots in the park. On cold winter Michigan days, he bribed them by promising hot chocolate as an incentive.

The habit of daily drills and shots cultivated stability in the midst of all the changes occurring in Sugar's life. While he might have reacted to all the family drama surrounding him by joining a gang or doing drugs, he was a good student and stayed out of trouble. Still, he grins. "I got my homework done, but I was always thinking about basketball, basketball, basketball." Plus, Bobbie watched him like a hawk in case he ever did mess up!

One of their next-door neighbors was a white family of Dutch immigrants. They chose to remain in the neighborhood rather than flee from the black families moving in. The mother, whose name happened to be Grace like the McLaughlins' younger daughter, had quickly become good friends with Mary Ruth. Sugar recalls thinking that his new neighbors spoke with a cool accent. Their son and daughter taught him how to ice skate at King Park. After Mary Ruth died, the bond formed between the McLaughlins and their Dutch neighbors became even tighter. They became more like a family than mere neighbors.

In addition, while their dad was working two jobs to make ends meet, a family friend, Miss Tarlee Jenkins, often came to the house. She helped Sugar's younger nephews and nieces get ready for school. Eventually, they started calling her Mom. But Sugar, out of respect for his mom, always referred to her as Miss Jenkins. No one could replace his mom. Instead, basketball became his surrogate.

For basketball was conveniently affordable, given the financial constraints on the family. He just needed a ball and a basket (or two, for full court play). He didn't need expensive equipment or clothes, just a decent pair of shoes. He could play year-round, indoors and outdoors, anywhere, anytime. All he had to do was head to the nearest basketball court or open gym.

A regulation game requires at least five members on each team. Players didn't necessarily need the required number to compete on the playgrounds or gyms. In *The In-Your-Face-Basketball Book,* Chuck Wielgus, Jr. and Alexander Wolff write on the culture of pick-up basketball. They describe the convenience of basketball. After all, when you go courting, there are "Games to play, from One-on-None 'til when day's done."[1]

Game Variations

One-on-None: Sugar could play basketball by himself for hours. He could hone his game by using imaginary players to simulate a real game.

One-on-One: With an additional player, he could test his moves in a game of one-on-one, and prove himself a defensive stopper. Also, a game of one-on-one was a great way to practice shooting and ball-handling skills, as well as prepare for an actual game of five-on-five.

Two-on-Two: Together with several players, Sugar could play a game of two-on-two and use the pick and roll, pick'n'pop, give and go, watch for chances to double-team an opponent, and look to get rebounding position on the weak side of the court, away from the ball.

Three-on-Three: Add a couple more players, and Sugar could engage in a 3-on-3 half-court match up. He could set picks on or away from the ball, run crisscross patterns, and set up a three-man, give-from-one-side-go-from-the-other-side back-door. As a guard, he practiced penetrating the lane, leaning to pass and screening away from his pass.

Four-on-Four: In a four-on-four game, Sugar would develop added court sense and awareness. Plus, he could sharpen the ability to get his shot off, learn to cope with contact, and polish his passing skills.

Five-on-Five: In full-court five-on-five games, he could prove he belonged, leading his team on a good run on the court. If not, he could discover weaknesses in his own game.

Traditionally, the winning team holds court and gets to ask the triumphant question, "Who's next?" challenging the next five players to try and beat them.

Various shooting games showed off his shooting range. Examples include H-O-R-S-E, Around the World, Twenty-one, Five-Three-One, Sets and Taps, Seven-Up, Knock-out, Scuttle-butt, Fight Twenty-one, and Fouls.

Sugar easily learned the fundamentals involved in basketball (e.g., dribble, shoot, pass, rebound, playing defense) while at the same time working to improve them. As an added bonus, basketball gave him all-around motivation. The sport challenged him to take care of his health, keep up his grades, stay out of trouble, and avoid the dangers of illegal drugs. Finally, as he has discovered over the years, basketball is a game that can be played for life. If you end up in a wheelchair someday, you can even play from there. For Sugar, basketball is not just a sport but is an integral part of his lifestyle. Throughout the many changes in Sugar's six decades of living on this earth, basketball has been a constant in his life.

Losing his mom at such a young age was a big blow for Melvin. Even today he grieves over her death, and wonders how his life might have turned out differently had she been around. Linda has been Melvin's faithful companion, since they first met in high school. She divulges,

 He's not the type to open up about his mom's passing away. His way to keep his mind off his loss was to go to the gym and play basketball. Sometimes he would express his anger, that she was taken away too early from him and things would have been different if she had been around. Basketball isn't just a game for him. I think it's how he deals with life's lows and his mom dying when he was so young.

As a Christian, Sugar is comforted in the hope of the resurrection and looks forward to being reunited with his mom in heaven one day. Meanwhile, on the court he has found a foretaste of that heavenly reunion. If heaven is a playground, as Zechariah 8:5 implies, then Melvin can be connected with his mom while still on this earth, whenever he's playing ball.

"We are surrounded by a cloud of witnesses," Hebrews 12:1 says. Perhaps the saints in heaven can observe us who are on this globe. If so, then Mary Ruth McLaughlin is no doubt cheering on her baby boy from a front row in paradise. She certainly insisted he be called by his given name of Melvin while she lived. Still, she might even join the rest of his fans in heaven and on earth by shouting, "Shoot it, Sugar!"

In Genesis 28, the patriarch Jacob had a dream of angels ascending and descending on a ladder. He called the place Bethel, meaning "House of God." God had assured him at that place He was with him. In a similar sense, the basketball court has been a Bethel for Sugar, a place where he can meet God and God can meet him and reassure him of His presence. Though his mom is no longer with him on earth, he hadn't been forsaken. God is with him. The courts and playgrounds where he's played have served as hallowed ground, sanctuaries, and temples of recreation in his life. They have provided a place of refuge and solace, shaped his identity, and been a means for him to make lifelong friends.

In spite of the long shadow of his mother's death on the McLaughlin household, Sugar has found joy on the basketball court. He's powered to light up the gym and the playgrounds.

Fred Stabley is famous for giving Earvin Johnson the nickname "Magic" while working for the *Lansing State Journal*. He would go on to become the sports information director at Central Michigan. He remarks, "The two greatest smiles in Michigan basketball are Magic Johnson's and Sugar McLaughlin's." While Magic's fast break style and passing prestidigitation brought joy to the game, Sugar has brought his own joy with his size- and distance-defying plays. There, he exudes a contagious happiness.

Bob Becker was the sports editor of *The Grand Rapids Press.* He recalls his first impression of Sugar, when watching him play as a sophomore for Creston. "I remember thinking the first time I saw him that he was a smile with a kid attached to it."[2] He continues,

> There have been so many great kids to come through the City League, and for 30 years I saw most of them. But my fondest memories also will be my first. Watching that skinny kid from Creston glide down the floor, then pull up, and with a slight fade away from the basket, bury another jumper from 25 feet away. His smile as he headed down court lit up the building. Sugar was as sweet as it got for me.[3]

Bobbie recalls watching his little brother play in high school, when people shook their heads in disbelief and elbowed each other. "Lord have *mercy!*" "Did you just see that?" Even on those gym bleachers in a public venue, maybe they were acknowledging the God Thing instilled in his little brother as a four-year-old, chasing that basketball down a gravel-paved driveway in Ann Arbor.

Jamaal Al-Din, speaking with a voice of awe and reverence, testifies, "We were blessed by God to have seen him play!"

10

IT TAKES A TEAM TO RAISE A PLAYER

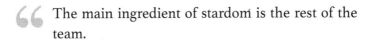 The main ingredient of stardom is the rest of the team.

— JOHN WOODEN

The African Proverb, "It takes a village to raise a child," suggests that raising children requires, along with their own parents, the love and care of others in the community. Since basketball is a team sport, this saying might be rephrased: "It takes a team to raise a player." Though Sugar lost a key teammate in his mom, God has blessed him with some outstanding teammates to assist him in the game of life. They played a role in making him a stupendous basketball player. But more importantly, they have assisted him in becoming a highly respected role model in the community. Everyone needs a team, and Sugar's teammates include family members, friends, coaches, and community leaders.

Family Members

Bobbie

In Sugar's life, the MVP Award goes to his oldest brother Bobbie, who remains one of his biggest supporters and fans. Ever since his mother extracted that deathbed promise, Bobbie has made sure his younger brother has stayed on the right path. If Sugar was ever tempted to go astray, Bobbie never hesitated to let him know right from wrong. Sometimes Sugar called him Mr. Enforcer. "My big brother always schooled me on the do's and don'ts of the streets in inner-city life." Fortunately, Bobbie says, the task wasn't as challenging as it could have been.

 As Melvin grew and matured into himself, I could see that I didn't have to worry as much as I had thought. He was just a good person. It was in his DNA. He didn't get too crazy or overboard with anything. He kept everything in moderation on his own. Of course, you're always going to need a little advice here and there. He did well. Our mom would be very proud of him. I'm sure she's smiling from heaven now. She would be very happy with the person he's turned out to be.

Bobbie became Mr. Everything to Sugar, and he kept his promise to his mother. Mel Atkins, Sugar's Middle School coach and the former athletic director of the Grand Rapids City League, says, "His brother just worshipped Melvin. Yes, Bobbie's a good one." Sugar laughs at that, adding, "He was also my biggest critic. I could have 40 points and he'd say, 'You could have had 45 points if you hadn't missed those five free throws!'"

During Sugar's jersey retirement ceremony at Central Michigan University's Rose Arena, the two brothers frequently wiped away tears as they looked upward. Hanging high above them was a maroon and gold banner inscribed with Melvin's name, uniform Number 14, and the years 1979-83. Afterward, Bobbie fought back even more tears. "I was his mentor. My mom told me ... to make sure Melvin got an education. Well, he got more than an education. He accomplished so much more here. That's why this day is just so beautiful."[1]

Bobbie McLaughlin Sr.

As he's gotten older, Sugar has grown to appreciate even more how his father dealt with the deaths of his wife and older daughter. They were "his two favorite ladies in the world." Being the sole provider and disciplinarian may have caused his dad to be a little too strict at times. Still, Sugar thanks God for how his dad not only fulfilled his role as a father, but grandfather as well, particularly in raising his sister Patricia's kids. As a father and, more recently, a grandfather himself, he is more thankful than ever that God gave him the dad he did.

Their father had a heart for the underdog, and though he was a hunter, the dog he chose was a pipsqueak of a pup with a ferocious bark. "The dog thought he was the biggest, baddest dog in the neighborhood," Bobbie says, laughing. "My dad loved that about him. Like my dad, Pepe had the biggest heart in the neighborhood."

They were people of honor, and Bobbie Sr. had lived through the horrors of growing up black in a white southern world. He and his brothers often swapped stories, and he kept his eye on the tension in the Grand Rapids community. During his own growing up years, Sugar had to deal with the changes in race relations. For example, he was transferred to a predominantly white school district, as result of desegregation. Sugar's dad advised him on how to respond respectfully should his skin color ever become an issue. To this day, Sugar sees people not in terms of their color but in terms of their humanity.

Along with raising him to be a gentleman, Bobbie Sr. wisely steered his younger son away from furthering his football career beyond Rocket League football. He also warned Sugar to eschew the suspect universities recruiting him in high school. Attending those schools could have resulted in life-altering consequences. A primary reason Sugar chose Central Michigan was its proximity to Grand Rapids. His dad could attend his home games, just a ninety-minute drive to Mount Pleasant.

An additional perk, however, to that choice was the location of the family freezer. His dad kept it stocked with game from his hunting trips. When Sugar returned to college after a visit home, his dad always looked at Bobbie and said, "Junior, can you check that freezer? I think the lock might be broken." Sure enough, Sugar had raided the stash for steaks to grill for his buddies back at Central.

Nephews and Nieces

Sugar's nephews and nieces retrieved his shots when they were younger. As they got older, some of his nephews joined him as teammates or opponents at the gym or playground. But his nephews and nieces didn't just help sharpen his basketball skills. They also motivated him to be a positive example for them to follow as their youngest uncle. One nephew, Bobbie's son Eric, went on to a hall of fame career at Akron University. He played a few years in the Continental Basketball Association. Eric's son and Bobbie's grandson, Michael, would continue the family's basketball legacy by making the Grand Rapids all-area team in high school and playing for Cornerstone University from 2013-2017.

Bobbie's other son Quinn, and Quinn's cousin Nick, both played high school ball. They now work as school counselors at East Kentwood High School and help out with their uncle Mel's annual basketball camp. Nick's brother Dobbie helps out whenever he's in town. In addition, Sugar's nieces, Tami, Renee, and Angala (Gracie's daughter), assist with the camp in any way they can. They can be found getting ice for injured players, helping out with registration, and making sure everyone is cared for, campers and guests alike. This family puts a new spin on "family camp" at Sugar Mel's Sweet Shot Basketball Camp!

Being a Father and "Paw Paw"

Having a son, daughter, and now grandkids has further helped Sugar mature as a man of God and community leader. He and Linda have a son, Melvin (aka "Little Sugar" or "Pooh"), and a daughter, Morgan, in addition to two grandchildren. Linda comments, "He's great with the grandkids. Before he was still into himself and basketball."

Son Melvin also played basketball at Creston, like his father. But he never felt pressured by his dad for stardom. "He just wanted me to love the game as much as he did." He says of his dad, "He's very wise. What more can I say? He's taught me how to be a father, because I have two little girls myself. He's an all-around good guy. Is he a better grandfather? He's still trying to adjust to that. He doesn't want to be called a grandfather yet, because he feels he's still young, so my kids just call him Paw Paw."

Additional Family Members

Sugar's mom had two sisters and one brother. His dad grew up in a family of eleven boys and three girls. Many are in heaven now. Clearly, Sugar was raised with the loving and rollicking support of lots of uncles and aunts, as well as numerous cousins. Their father's annual family Christmas celebration in Ann Arbor was one huge, boisterous, happy event. Anticipated all year long, they started planning the following year's party on the way home from the current reunion.

In addition, their dad had two other sons, Marshall Suttles and Michael Hughbanks, before meeting their mom, giving him two older half-brothers. Suttles died in 2019 and Hughbanks died in March of 2021. Sugar's close-knit circle of family and friends joined him at the retirement ceremony of his jersey number at Central Michigan.[2] In reflection, Sugar shakes his head in wonder and gratitude. His family has been able to stick together through thick and thin. In spite of all they've been through, the love they have for each other has only become stronger.

Friends

Tony Winston

Some key friends in Sugar's life include Tony Winston, Linda Chandler, and Bennette Gay. Tony's family was one of the few black families on their block when the McLaughlins first moved to Prince Street. Tony and he played ball together at Franklin/King Park and eventually became teammates in Middle School and High School.

When Sugar was selected to play for the Michigan All-Stars during his junior and senior years in high school, Tony drove to Detroit with him after classes in order to practice with the rest of the All-Stars at St. Cecilia's gym. The following morning, they both had to fight off the urge to sleep in rather than get up for class.

Tony died of cancer at age 49 in 2011, but he played no small role in Sugar's life. Besides being a loyal friend, he also introduced him to the person who would become the main woman in his life, Linda Chandler. Around ten years later, in 1989, Tony was with them in the hospital when Linda was about to give birth to their first child. Linda remembers Tony saying to her during labor, "Hurry up, so Melvin and I can go celebrate and have a drink." She says with her dry humor, "And that's the last thing you want to hear when you're in labor."

Linda Chandler

Tony first introduced Linda Chandler and Sugar, during Sugar's senior year. Linda was a sophomore and Junior Varsity cheerleader for Union High School. Union's Red Hawks were one of Creston's rivals in the Grand Rapids City League. Even though she cheered, Linda wasn't really into basketball. She'd never even seen Sugar play. She'd heard about him, though, especially through her friend Dee Dee. Before meeting Sugar, as far as she was concerned, he was just another basketball player at Creston High School. As she recalls,

 It was like a joke of mine as to how I was introduced to Melvin. Actually, Tony liked me at first, but he didn't realize that I was younger. In high school at the time, it was a big deal to date someone who was two to three years older than you. When Tony found out I was younger, he asked if I had an older sister and if I did, he should have met her, instead. He kind of hurt my feelings. I said as a comeback, "Well then, I should have met Melvin McLaughlin, instead!"

After a game between Union and Creston, Linda was sitting with Dee Dee at the Burger King near Michigan and Fuller. Tony and Sugar walked in. Introducing Sugar to Linda, Tony said, "She wants to meet you."

Linda was so embarrassed she balked, "No, I don't want to meet him!" But eventually they exchanged numbers. Linda comments, "The big joke around school was that I was dating a senior!" Sugar was nearly three years older than Linda, but they've been a couple ever since.

Sugar's winning smile, pleasant personality, and basketball popularity caught the attention of a lot of ladies at Creston and Central Michigan. But Linda has remained a bedrock in his life. She reflects, "I think the reason why I was so attractive to Melvin was that I was more interested in him as a person than just a basketball player." After Sugar got cut from the NBA, she adds,

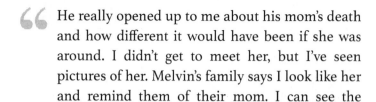

He really opened up to me about his mom's death and how different it would have been if she was around. I didn't get to meet her, but I've seen pictures of her. Melvin's family says I look like her and remind them of their mom. I can see the resemblance in the color, hair, and cheekbones.

After meeting Linda in person, it's clear why she won Sugar's heart. Not only is she outwardly beautiful, her love for Sugar and others is evident. When watching her work at the registration table, some of the younger volunteers gravitated to her like an older sister. And the even younger volunteers, like a mother. Her eyes light up when she sees Melvin Junior walking towards her with her beautiful two granddaughters. Arms extended, they dash up to receive her hugs and kisses.

When talking about Sugar and his life, she glows. She gets him! She understands just how important basketball is to her man. And so, she has a special tolerance for the hours he spends on the court and his passion for the game. She's not there to compete with his love for the game. She's there to complete him in his love for the game. Her respect for Sugar is reciprocated by Sugar's respect for her. As one of the most popular figures in Grand Rapids, Sugar receives a lot of phone calls. He can't possibly answer them right away and sometimes, he'll choose to ignore them, especially if they're from a number he doesn't recognize. But when Linda calls, he picks up immediately. Even if he happens to be in the middle of playing basketball!

Bennette Gay

As a sophomore at Creston, Sugar got to know Bennette when he was a senior. Sugar was labeled "The Super Sophomore" coming off the bench that year. Both share a bond in their mutual love for basketball and have similar mild demeanors. Bennette went on to play at Eastern Michigan

University. He ended up coaching at Central, Ottawa Hills, Creston, and Union High Schools in the Grand Rapids City League. Sugar's son played for Bennette at Creston, and Sugar became Bennette's assistant. He also assisted Bennette with coaching at Union. Occasionally, they teamed up again in the Gus Macker 3 on 3 Tournaments and while playing for Sugar Mel's All-Star team. Bennette is a regular contributor at Sugar Mel's Basketball Camp. Similar to Sugar, you'd never guess by his mild demeanor that Bennette had been one of the top players in the Grand Rapids' City League. I can't picture him doing a lot of screaming when he coached. When I asked him about his coaching style, he affirmed this by saying, "Yelling and screaming doesn't work. You have to show respect for the kids for them to respect you." When Bennette married, Sugar stood up as his best man. As Linda shares, "If you asked Melvin about his best friend growing up, it was always Tony. But later on, I'd say his closest friend would be Bennette."

Additional Teammates

Sugar was bolstered by fellow teammates at Central Michigan. Sonny Newman, Kim Thompson (aka "KT") and Derek Boldon provided mutual support and camaraderie during their up-and-down years at Central. They often prayed together when things got tough. The four remained friends and supporters of each other, long after they last donned a golden and maroon Chippewa uniform. Sadly KT died in June of 2021.

Other ball players and coaches assist Sugar with his camp. Anthony Gordon played for Kentwood in high school, Indiana Tech in college, and later on Sugar Mel's All-Star team. Additional assistance comes from Creston standout and former Forest Hills Eastern Varsity Girls coach, Steven "Preacher" Lee; and fellow Creston classmate and East Kentwood's Junior Varsity Boys Basketball coach, Robert Roelofs.

Community Leaders in Grand Rapids

Grand Rapids Tackers

Sugar watched some of the marquee NBA and college players play on TV. He also had the advantage of seeing the Grand Rapids Tackers play live and in person. Most games were played at Godwin Heights High School in the southwest suburb of Wyoming. Occasionally they played at the Civic Center downtown, or at Wyoming's Rogers High School. Some of their games ended up being "turn-away" games. Due to the limited size of their playing facility, all the fans couldn't be admitted.[3]

The team's colors of orange and black corresponded to the traditional colors of a basketball. But they could be seen as a nod to Ottawa Hills High School's colors. "The 'O'" was known for its predominantly black athletic teams and were the Class A State Basketball Champions in 1968 and 1969. A euphemism for a hard worker, the nickname Tackers stems from Grand Rapids' reputation as the Furniture Capital of the World.

The NBA was much smaller back then, and many top college players never made the pro rosters. If you were black, you also had to overcome an unofficial barrier. Teams limited the number of black players who could wear their uniforms. Herschel Turner explains, "Back in my day only three (black) guys could play on a team. This was even in high school."[4]

Their only option was to play for teams like the Tackers, where they would make a couple of hundred dollars playing at high school gymnasiums. They competed in relative obscurity and for low pay. But pay grade and fame do not make or break talent. The Tackers were remarkable, usually scoring over 100 points per game! Bob Becker remarks, "I saw a program for one of those games and that year (1972-1973) they had one guy who averaged 39.1 points a game, (Steve) Mix averaged 31.1, and a third guy averaged over 27 points a game.

Basically, they had three guys averaging better than 90 points a game."

The Tackers won the Midwest Professional Basketball League in 1963-1964, and the North American Basketball League Championship in 1964-1965 and 1967-1968. They finished their franchise's final season in grand fashion in 1974-1975. After going 23-3 in the regular season, they went on to become the International Basketball League Champions.

During their years of existence, the Tacker roster was consistently filled with local and national legendary players such as Bill "the Hill" McGill, Willie "The Bird" Jones, Nick "Praying" Mantis, Hershell Turner, Bob Wilkinson, George Knighton, Don Edwards, Marcellus Starks, The Robinsons (Mike and Flynn), the Burton brothers (M.C. and Ed), and the Carlisle brothers (Elmo and Clarence).

As William Bushnell describes, "Most of the players were black with huge bodies and remarkable skills totally different from us white-bred Dutch kids," but as good as they were, "most were frustrated, even depressed players who were destined not to make the big-time money."[5]

Not only could Sugar watch the Tackers shine on the court, he got to know many of the Tackers in the community, such as George Knighton and Hershell Turner at the Baxter Community Center, Ernie Johnson at Campau Park, Delton Heard at the Paul I. Philips Recreation Center, and Don Edwards at Creston High School. At Grand Rapids Central, Elmo Carlisle did some assistant coaching in the area. He offered tips to up-and-coming players while playing recreational ball. Looking back, Clarence Carlisle, Elmo's brother, says,

 We didn't really think it was anything special we were doing. Giving back to the community was just part of who we were as players and a team. We didn't make a lot of money playing and we

certainly didn't make a lot of money working in the community. But it wasn't about the money. It was about giving back to others what we received when we were growing up. We were just paying it forward.

The Tackers served as role models for Sugar not only on the court. Even more significantly, off the court they gave back to the community of Grand Rapids. Their generous presence was not wasted on the kid with the wild shot from the back of the court.

Johnny Walker and Rex Jones

Two other standouts in the community who have assisted Sugar in developing his basketball career and character include long-time family friends Johnny Walker and Rex Jones. Walker is the nephew of the late Ted Rasberry, a longtime advocate of Grand Rapids inner-city youth. In 1935, Rasberry moved to Grand Rapids from Mississippi, and died in 1981 at 89. A former player, he was manager and/or owner of multiple teams. The lineup included the Grand Rapids Black Sox, Detroit Stars and Kansas City Monarchs baseball teams. Eventually, one of Rasberry's nieces, Minnie Forbes, became the owner of the Stars.[6]

Walker once played for the Detroit Stars, KC Monarchs, and GR Black Sox. For eighteen years he coached girls basketball at Union High School. He first witnessed Sugar play when he was a security guard at Iroquois Middle School. At the time, Walker worked for the Grand Rapids' Park and Recreation Department. He creatively offered Sugar a job that matched his basketball pursuits. He would pay him, if he would keep the basketball courts at King Park clean and shoot a minimum of one hundred shots a day. Sugar had no problem meeting the job requirements and more.

Jones, like Walker, is a fellow youth advocate and former

Negro League Baseball player. He played for the Los Angeles Braves and Indianapolis Clowns. He also joined the Kansas City Monarchs during their 1964 barnstorming season alongside Odell Daniels, Leroy Doster and Satchel Page. In 1966, he was in spring training with the California Angels. After his baseball playing days were over in 1967, Jones joined Rasberry by working for the Harlem Satellites basketball team. Rasberry had conceived the idea of organizing the finest black basketball talent available. His goal was to make the game more appealing for all members of the family, young and old. He combined the talented players with the most well-established comedy performers into one traveling unit. Rasberry signed Bill "Rookie" Brown in 1956 as his player-coach. They made it their mission to pluck the best talent available and started to search for exhibition matches. Over the next 30 years, Jones played, coached, promoted, and booked games for the Harlem Satellites, Harlem Thrillers, Travelers and Global Trotters. They played their last game in Las Vegas, New Mexico (not to be confused with Las Vegas, Nevada) in 2003.[7]

Together with Rasberry, Jones helped establish the GAP (Grow, Achieve, Progress) program and inner-city baseball in Grand Rapids. Walker and Jones still live in the neighborhood. The former Negro Leaguers were part of the dedication ceremony of the newly revitalized Rasberry Field, 1010 Sheldon Street SE, in 2016. Rasberry Field was one of eight fields to be utilized for the Grand Rapids YMCA free Inner-City Youth Baseball/Softball program.[8]

Even now, Jones and Walker can be found on the sidelines at Sugar Mel's Basketball Camp. They support Sugar's efforts as seasoned veterans in reaching out to Grand Rapids' inner-city youth through sports. Jones comments, "I thought he was going to make it in the NBA, but you never know in the sports business. God has him right where he's at though, working with the kids. I'm proud of him."

Additional Community Members

To ensure that Sugar continues to achieve his goal of an affordable camp where no player is turned away due to a lack of funds, a variety of sponsors in the community generously provide their support. In Mark 2:1-12, four men were carrying their paralyzed friend to Jesus but were unable to do so because of the crowd. Undeterred, they made a hole in the roof above and lowered their friend to Jesus. Similarly, these camp sponsors have networked together in order to make sure that no financial barrier will get in the way of a child being blessed from knowing and learning from Grand Rapids' greatest player of all time.

Bobbie and Sugar give thanks to God for the way all of the sponsors have come together to support their annual Sugar Mel's All-Star Basketball Camp in reaching out to the children in the community of Grand Rapids. You know who you are!

Sugar and his family also benefit from the support and prayers of extended church family. New Hope Baptist Church is located on the southwest side of Grand Rapids. Several members can be spotted volunteering at his summer basketball camp.

Coaches

Never underestimate the long-term impact of a good coach. Sugar appreciates the guidance and mentoring he received from caring coaches with whom he continues to maintain close relationships today.

Mel Atkins and Jim Haskins

In hindsight, Sugar realizes how blessed he was to have Mel Atkins and Jim Haskins as his coaches. They allowed him to express his individual talents on the playing floor. "A lot of coaches, especially back then, don't let you do that. They'll take you out if you shoot from far outside rather than working the ball inside, or if you do a behind-the-back pass. I was fortunate to have Coach Atkins in middle school and Coach Haskins in high school."

Atkins and Haskins have more in common than having coached one the greatest outside shooters in basketball history. Both are proud alumni of Grand Rapids South High School. And they have been leaders in seeing to the success of practically every athlete and program in the area.

Atkins was the Grand Rapids City League's athletic director for 25 years. He and Sugar have remained close, since they first met at Iroquois Middle School in 1973-1974. His nephew Chuck Ruffin is a retired football coach at Ottawa Hills. He says, "People have no idea how many good things Melvin Atkins has done for athletics and athletes in the Grand Rapids Public Schools and the City League." Ruffin had lived with his uncle and his family in high school. He adds, "They haven't seen him give kids rides when they didn't have a way to get to school, or go in his pocket to pay for some kid to take a college entrance exam."[9] Overseeing the City League Athletics, Atkins often put his family vacations on hold to help the athletes in the city.

Haskins, Sugar's coach at Creston, says of Atkins, "He did a lot of things behind the scenes to help kids, including kids I coached, whether it was guidance or directions, or to get in their face to make sure the kid was doing the right thing—he was doing that, even back in the 1970s. He's always been there to help the kids."[10]

Atkins is a regular visitor of Sugar's camp, and from time to time Atkins and Sugar catch up over a meal. As he describes, "He always greets me with a big hug. We go way back." It's no surprise that, towards his retirement, Atkins helped the City League team members make a smooth transition into the Ottawa-Kent County Conference in 2008-2009—headed by Melvin's high school coach, Jim Haskins.

Coach Haskins started teaching at Creston in 1969-1970,

coaching football and later basketball. After leaving Creston in 1982, he served as principal of Rockford High School, helping achieve the school's vision by upgrading its technology for the 21st century. Later, he was the original commissioner of the OK Conference in West Michigan. By 2019, the OK Conference consisted of seven different leagues and 49 schools, when Haskins retired after 12 years.[11] In 2018, Haskins was inducted into the Grand Rapids Sports Hall of Fame and was awarded the Warren Reynolds Lifetime Achievement Award.[12]

Similar to Atkins, Haskins helped the city kids transition to the Creston neighborhood. The Grand Rapids Public School Board had closed South High and chose to integrate Union, Creston and Central. Ottawa Hills was already considered integrated. By the time Sugar enrolled in Creston, things were going pretty smoothly.

Haskins credits both the administration and Sugar in handling the desegregation process at Creston well. As he reflects,

> Everybody was proactive, and we had a good cross section of teachers. Seven or eight teachers on the staff, including myself, had gone to South or had been teaching at South. It also helped to have Melvin as a student and leader at Creston. He's just a likable guy. I never had any problem with him on or off the court. Some of the racial tension at Creston was real, but some was exaggerated to be much larger than it really was. For most of the kids, when you're playing the game, the only color that matters is the color of the uniform.

On the court, Haskins sought to capitalize on Sugar's shooting ability, giving him the green light to shoot at least 20 to 25 times a game. Looking back on Sugar's career at Creston,

Haskins says, "What he did was no fluke. I saw it for three years, year around, even in open gyms. We saw more of him in practice than people saw in the games."

As with Coach Atkins, Haskins and his former star player remain close to this day. He says proudly, "My kids absolutely love him. My granddaughter loves him. And she's going to his camp this year. She's seen him play in the Mackers and all that. He's giving back to the community and that's what's great!"

Dave Ginsberg

As assistant coach for the Chippewas from 1975-1991, Dave Ginsberg played a pivotal role in signing Sugar for Central Michigan. Gins matches Melvin's enthusiasm for basketball and for life. Ginsberg is known as "The White Shadow of Michigan basketball." *The White Shadow* was a TV drama series that aired from 1978 to 1981. Ken Howard (aka "The White Shadow") portrayed a fictional former NBA player, who ends up coaching at an inner-city high school in Los Angeles.

Ginsberg, now in his mid 70s, coached basketball at the high school and collegiate level for 40 seasons spread out over six decades. In addition to a 16-year stint as an assistant coach at CMU (1975-1991), he coached either boys' or girls' programs in eight different high schools. A lot of coaches like to impress upon their players how good they were when they played, as if that will add to their respect. I never heard Gins once talk about his glory days as a player. I had to prod him to learn that he played in high school and on the freshman team at Central Michigan.

Instead, I've heard him say over and over, just what a blessing and honor it was to have worked with such wonderful young people. And of all the players he's coached, I can tell he has a special affinity for Sugar! During my initial interview with Dave, I mentioned I was staying at my dad's house. He grew quiet, then told me what a blessing it was for me to still have my dad. Later he shared that when he was a freshman at

Central Michigan, his dad died. He still remembers how some of the players on the team came to his dorm to inform him of the news. And how the coaches and his teammates became like a family to him that year, to help him cope with his grief.

Ever since, he's been trying to instill a family atmosphere among the players and coaching staff wherever he has been, including Central Michigan. Knowing that Sugar experienced the loss of his mom at such a young age, Gins realized how important being a part of such a family was for Sugar, especially when he was away from Grand Rapids.

In the process of my writing this book, Ginsberg has generously offered constructive criticism, urging me to highlight just what a wonderful person Sugar is, even more so than even his basketball ability. He's gone out of his way to help me connect with numerous interviewees that on my own, there's no way I could have had an audience with. From outer appearances, there's nothing slick or disingenuous about him. To paraphrase what Jesus said about Nathaniel in John 1:47, "He is a true coach in whom there is no guile!"

When he speaks, his love and passion for basketball and for today's youth is completely transparent. He wears his heart on his sleeve and doesn't hold anything back in pouring out his emotions. No wonder he was able to get Sugar to play for him! I would have run through a brick wall, if I had played under him. Ginsberg was inducted into the Basketball Coaches Association of Michigan Hall of Honor in 2016, and into the National High School Basketball Coaches Association Court of Honor the following year.

Ginsberg first met the McLaughlins when Sugar was in middle school. He drove down from Central Michigan's campus to see him play, always putting a bug in his ear about playing for him in Mount Pleasant someday. His integrity and loyalty proved to be the key factor in Sugar's decision to play for the Chippewas.

He attempted to sell the benefits of being a part of the Chippewa basketball program in various ways. He named the NBA players who had once donned a Chippewa uniform (like Ben Kelso, Jim McElroy, Dan Roundfield, and Ben Poquette). He extolled the players from the Grand Rapids area who had played or were playing for Central. That list included John Berends, Don Edwards, Val Bracey, and Leon Guydon. Plus, they'd be so close that his family members could attend his games. Then there was the beauty of the campus and quality of its academics. He listed some of the fellow recruits who would be joining Sugar at Central Michigan in the fall (e.g., James Koger, Rob McQuaid, and Gary Tropf).

Ultimately, what really sealed the deal for Sugar eventually signing with Central? Ginsberg's promise to always be there for him, even after his playing days for the Chippewas were over.

Ginsberg has been faithful in keeping his promise. To paraphrase Proverbs 18:24, "He is a coach who sticks closer than a brother." Like Sugar and me, he is a lifelong basketball enthusiast. His passionate motivational speeches are a highlight of Sugar Mel's Basketball Camp. The kids are inspired not just to succeed on the playing floor but off the playing floor, as well. Like a White Shadow, these lessons will follow them the rest of their lives.

Ginsberg currently serves as the secretary/treasurer of the National High School Basketball Coaches Association. He remains a beloved figure in the basketball circles wherever he has coached and taught.

Dick Parfitt

Sugar's head coach at Central Michigan University, Dick Parfitt, was an old-school coach. He wasn't accustomed to a player with such a long shooting range. So, at first, he didn't fully utilize Sugar's arsenal. Soon, however, he realized the benefits of putting the ball in Sugar's hands. Once Number 14 crossed half court, Parfitt greenlighted him. Parfitt says,

He was just tremendous when he was here. Melvin wasn't surrounded by our best players here. He missed them by a few years, but he carried us. When we did something good, it was because he carried us. If they would have had the three-point play then, he would have been phenomenal. He had a green light, believe me. At the end of the game, he always had the ball in his hands, and made a lot of winning buckets for us.

God Is Melvin's Head Coach

Above all, Sugar looks to God as his lifelong Head Coach, both on and off the playing floor. He sees basketball as God's gift, making sure to give Him the credit for his ability to play the game. Just as he coaches his campers, Sugar strives to be a wise steward. He uses the gift of basketball as a means to reach out to the community. As he acknowledged after his camp in 2017, "I'd like to take this time to give thanks and to show appreciation to the grace of God Almighty. He has blessed me by putting me in a very special position to give back to the community in a very special way. That is through the gift of basketball."[13]

11

MIDDLE SCHOOL PHENOM

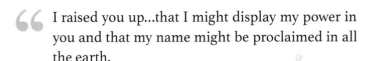 I raised you up...that I might display my power in you and that my name might be proclaimed in all the earth.

— Romans 9:17

By 1973, when Sugar suited up for Iroquois Middle School as a seventh grader, he had developed a cult-like following. Word of mouth continued to spread about this "little kid they call 'Sugar' who could shoot the lights out." Only they weren't just being drawn to Sugar only. They were also gathered like moths to the flame of God's glory shining through him on the basketball floor. He fulfills the challenge in Matthew 5:16, "Let your light shine before others, that they may see your good deeds and glorify your Father in heaven." He represented heaven's playground not only in how he played but in the way he played with unspeakable joy.

Sugar was already a bona fide playground icon in Grand Rapids. His legendary status accelerated even without the aid of today's social media outlets, smartphone videos, self-promotion blogs, and YouTube Highlight mixes.

Back then, everything spread by word of mouth. People could not possibly keep to themselves his spectacular performances on the hardwood. Those who finally got a chance to witness for themselves Sugar's glorious feats on the playing floor often turned to those watching with them. "Did you just see what I saw?" "How could he possibly do that?" Were their eyes playing tricks on them or should they set up an appointment with an optometrist?

Sugar and his remarkable playing skills became a favorite topic among basketball fans. They couldn't stop talking about him at barber shops, church and school gatherings, sports bars, poker games, and other neighborhood hangouts.

There used to be a chain of family restaurants in West Michigan named Mr. Fables, known for its Olive Burgers and fried-battered onion rings. One of the tag-lines of Mr. Fables was "too good to be true." Sugar might have been a fitting spokesman for Mr. Fables when he played, for as word of mouth began to spread about his game and shooting range, like Mr. Fables advertised their food to be, it sounded too good to be true.

Talk extended in concentric circles to the outer limits of Grand Rapids. It rippled to the suburbs, and beyond. Basketball fans in the greater Grand Rapids area of different backgrounds, social classes, and races began to unite. They flocked to Sugar's games to verify what they were hearing. He would prove before their eyes that the rumors were true and in fact often even better than what they had heard over and over again.

During his entire middle school career, Sugar never lost a game. He began in seventh grade, playing for the Iroquois Middle School Braves. There in the Ottawa Hills School District, he started for the eighth grade A team, averaging 15 points a game. Middle school coach Atkins says, "He started for me as a seventh grader and we went undefeated. We beat the ninth-grade championship team that year. He was tremendous. I can't think of anybody from the Grand Rapids area that could shoot as well. What drew people to Melvin's games was seeing this kid fire the basketball up from all over the place."

Due to school integration, Sugar was bused his eighth- and ninth-grade years to Riverside Middle School. Riverside, more than five miles from home, was in the Creston School District on the northeast side of Grand Rapids. His former school was only a few blocks away. Still, in spite of potential problems, he easily and successfully shifted schools. The school board chose Coach Atkins to teach at Riverside, as a familiar face for the students transferring from Iroquois. Subsequently, Atkins handpicked Sugar to join him as a leader among his peers. Of course, he also looked forward to being reunited with his star player on the Riverside Cubs' basketball team.

As a leader in the school, Sugar easily made new friends at Riverside, and had no trouble transitioning to his new playing floor. While suiting up for the team as an eighth grader, Sugar's scoring average climbed to 20 points per game. His ninth-grade average of 38 points per game was the most by any ninth grader in the storied history of the Grand Rapids City League.[1]

In one game he scored an astonishing sixty points. Besides playing without a three-point line, Sugar's middle school games consisted of only four six-minute quarters. (High school games have four eight-minute quarters, college games have two 20-minute halves, and pro games consist of four 12-minute quarters.) If he maintained the same pace, he would have scored 80 points in high school, 100 in college, and 120 points in a professional game. And with the addition of the three-point line, he would have had even more!

Just as at Iroquois, Sugar would lead his team in back-to-back undefeated seasons at Riverside. Time and again he proved that he was as good as advertised, and oftentimes even better. Sugar's fan club continued to grow as others began to jump on the "Sugar Mel" bandwagon. His outstanding ability to shoot the lights out drew tides of people in to see his sweet shots. Afterward, they went out and exclaimed to others, "This kid Sugar is amazing! You should see him play!"

Former Union High School and Hope College basketball and baseball standout, John "Thunder" Klunder recalls first watching Sugar play in middle school. "Nobody has ever been better than Sugar. All the gyms were packed to see him play, from his ninth-grade year at Riverside Junior High, where my dad took me to one of his games, through his years at Creston, where they played their home games at Northeast Junior High School."

Klunder's friend, Todd Stacy, was a couple of grades ahead of him and in the same grade as Sugar. Stacy wasn't quite as enthusiastic about watching Sugar's radar-like bombs from the outside. The designated defensive stopper on the team, Stacy played for West Middle School and Union High. He was given the Sisyphean task of guarding Sugar throughout his middle school and high school career.

The most influential of Sugar's followers was the assistant coach of Central Michigan University. David Ginsberg had been a former coach at Grand Rapids' Union High School. Some of the city's basketball coaches and fans tipped him off about this kid called Sugar, who could drain long-range jumpers like no one they had ever seen.

His regular ninety-minute drive from Mount Pleasant for Sugar's games would eventually pay off. Even though recruited by over two hundred other schools, Sugar accepted a scholarship to play for Central Michigan University.

He attended the summer basketball camps of the state's two Big Ten schools, Michigan State University and the University of Michigan. Afterward, Sugar's reputation stretched beyond

Grand Rapids to Mount Pleasant, then to East Lansing and Ann Arbor. At both camps, Sugar received the Most Valuable Player award.

In eighth grade at Michigan's State's camp, Sugar competed against a player rated as the top eighth grader in the state. From Benton Harbor, he bore the nickname "The Grasshopper," presumably due to his jumping ability. Although his nickname could have also stemmed from a popular TV show at the time, *Kung Fu*, starring actor David Carradine. Carradine's character, Kwai Kai Caine, was nicknamed Grasshopper, while training to be a Shalom monk. Maybe this Benton Harbor phenom had been nicknamed The Grasshopper, because he was considered a superstar basketball player in training?

Whatever the reason for his nickname, when he went up against Sugar, The Grasshopper was so flustered (or in Sugar's words, "I destroyed him!") that he ended up in tears. He even challenged Sugar to a fight. Perhaps, he figured that if he couldn't beat Sugar on the basketball court, then he could beat him in a fistfight? Or, given his nickname, maybe he wanted to take Sugar on in a Kung-Fu duel?

Two Michigan State star players, Terry Furlow and Bobby Chapman, worked at the camp. They wanted to calm the highly regarded Grasshopper and give him an opportunity to save face. They invited Sugar and The Grasshopper to join them in a two-on-two battle. Before their match, Chapman and Furlow made a bet. Which eighth grader would outdo the other, Grasshopper or Sugar? Furlow teamed up with The Grasshopper and Chapman partnered with Sugar. Chapman won the bet as Sugar again totally exterminated The Grasshopper.

Whatever became of this potential leaping star is a mystery. It's possible that he continued to play ball for Benton Harbor sans his former nickname. Or maybe he was so decimated by Sugar that he gave up the game altogether? All we know is that by the time Sugar was in high school, there is no mention of a basketball player nicknamed Grasshopper on the roster of the Benton Harbor Tigers in the archives of the state's newspapers. Hopefully the lad pressed on with hoops, because everyone can grow from meeting a formidable challenger.

Meanwhile, Sugar continued to strut his stuff in his childhood town of Ann Arbor at the University of Michigan's basketball camp. There he also received the Most Valuable Player award. At the Wolverines' camp, he would meet one of his future teammates at Central Michigan. Derek Boldon, a couple of grades behind Melvin, recalls, "Since I was big for my age, I moved up to the older group right below the middle schoolers. Melvin was the MVP of the camp. We hit it off right away and just connected. We lost touch over the years, but then out of luck or should I say God's providence, we both ended up at Central."

Given his stellar performances in middle school, on the playgrounds, and in the gyms of Grand Rapids, Sugar stood out from the other players his age. His MVP showings at Michigan State's and the University of Michigan's basketball camps only elevated his reputation as a player to watch for in the future. By the time he enrolled at Creston, he was by far the most highly regarded sophomore in the area.

The expectations were high for the super sophomore with the smooth game and a megawatt smile to match his electrifying shooting ability. Unlike The Grasshopper, Sugar did not disappoint.

12

SHOOTING STAR FOR THE POLAR BEARS

❝ He would have scored a lot, lot of points, that's for sure. I dare say, if the 3-point shot was in effect, his stats would have been unbelievable.

— Bennette Gay (Sugar's teammate at Grand Rapids Creston High School)

Melvin's Grand Rapids Creston High School jersey was officially retired in 2006. But from 1976-1979, when he donned Number 15 for the Polar Bears, his shooting percentage was more torrid than arctic.

Sugar was on track to attend Ottawa Hills High School after Iroquois Middle School. Ottawa Hills had become the largest black school in Grand Rapids after South High closed in 1968. South High enrolled more minority students than any of the other Grand Rapids Public Schools. Nonetheless, the court declared the school guilty for lacking diversity in its teaching staff. As a result, beginning in the 1969-1970 school year, incoming South High senior class members were filtered to three different high schools in the city: Grand Rapids Central,

Grand Rapids Union, and Grand Rapids Creston.[1] Ottawa Hills was already considered integrated.

The desegregation efforts were mostly one way, with black students, like Sugar, being bused to predominantly white schools. Being forced to attend a school out of the neighborhood wasn't easy to take. As a former South High student asked, "Can't you achieve quality education and integration by busing white students into the inner city instead of busing black students into the outer city?"[2]

After graduating from Riverside Middle School, Sugar attended Creston High School from 1976-1979. During those years, the student body was around 20% black and 80% white.[3]

But Sugar had no problem fitting in, given his humble personality. He considers the racial percentages. "I never thought I was better than anyone else because I can play basketball, or that I had a gift that was better than anyone else's." Students of all backgrounds and colors cheered for Sugar and the rest of the sleuth of Polar Bears that played for Creston's varsity basketball team. They packed the North East Middle School gymnasium (1400 Fuller Avenue NE) where the Polar Bears played their home games.

Robert Roelofs, East Kentwood's junior varsity basketball coach, attended Creston's home games with his classmates. They found a common bond as members of the fan club of Grand Rapids' original one-man Polar Express. (East Grand Rapids' Chris Van Allsburg's best-selling children's book *The Polar Express* would not come out until 1985.) Roelofs says, "Each of us picked a number between twenty and sixty, predicting how many points Melvin would score, and put a dollar in the pot. The person who picked the correct number or who came closest to the number, would collect the money and then treat everybody to the McDonald's on Leonard Street afterward."

As a sophomore, Sugar was the sixth man on a varsity team

mostly comprised of seniors. First team included All-Stater Tim Bracey, 6'3", whose older brother Val at the time was starring for Central Michigan. In addition, Sugar would play alongside senior guard Bennette Gay, who became one of his closest friends. Bennette had transferred to Creston from the former South High District. During his senior year, he was nominated for the All-Area team and was honorable mention for the All-State team. He would go on to play for the Eastern Michigan University Hurons (now Eagles).

Sugar's initial high school season turned out to be his winningest at Creston. The Polar Bears' regular season record was 24 wins and one loss, going 12-0 in the City League. This ranked them second in the state heading into the Class A Michigan High School Athletic Association basketball tournament. They advanced to the Class A quarter finals before losing to the Saginaw Trojans in double overtime. Had they defeated Saginaw, they'd have played against Magic Johnson and his Lansing Everett Vikings in the semifinals.

Instead, Saginaw advanced to the final four, only to be upstaged by the Vikings. Magic then led Everett to the state finals against Kevin Smith's Birmingham Brother Rice. In dramatic fashion, the Lansing Everett Vikings would go on to win the 1977 Class A Championship in overtime. As Coach Jim Haskins reflects on his talented 1976-1977 squad, "We were very close. An official's call here and there and we would have been in the finals. It just wasn't supposed to be." In retrospect, many contend that the main reason Creston lost in the quarter finals was because Sugar didn't play enough in the game.

Although just a sophomore, Sugar played a key role in Creston's success, coming off the bench and averaging double figures. He also added depth to the backcourt of Bennette, Richard Magsby, and Mark Chanski. Already, he was becoming Coach's "go to" player in the crunch. In one game he started for a flu-stricken Gay, and made the most of the opportunity by scoring 18 points.[4]

Soon Sugar Fever began to spread throughout "The Polar Bear Nation," while causing migraines for the opposition. Dan Nilsen of *The Grand Rapids Press* wrote, after Sugar provided instant offense against West Catholic, "And little Melvin McLaughlin, the super soph who is fast becoming the darling of Creston fans, came off the bench and hit his first four shots in the second quarter en route to a 12-point performance."[5] Sugar's dazzling display of floor leadership helped Creston defeat Central for the third time of the year. This moved them to the Class A Regional finals. Coach Haskins disclosed, "I told the guys when it gets to that time of the game, give the ball to the little guy."[6]

Creston wasn't quite as talented during Sugar's junior and senior years. As the only returning varsity player, he had to get used to playing with the previous year's Junior Varsity players. But playing with less talented and unseasoned teammates had a silver lining. It allowed him to flourish as a player individually and express his unique talents on the court. Playing at a listed height and weight of 6'1" and 155 pounds, Sugar averaged better than 33 points a game in both his junior and senior years. During his three years at Creston, he averaged 25 points per game while totaling 1557 points.[7]

Early in Sugar's junior year, Creston suffered its first conference loss in over a year. Archrival Union soared over the defending City League champs, 73-56, in their conference opener. Mel still bombed in 28 points in a losing effort. Scott Scholten of *The Grand Rapids Press* wrote,

 With McLaughlin in the game, it's showtime. The slender guard with the long, dangling arms and huge hands moves around the court like he and the ball are waltz partners. He single-handedly

slithered through the Union press with several moves straight from the Earl Monroe handbook. Using his dazzling spins, he turned a one-on-three break into a twisting layup and brought the Creston fans to their feet.[8]

Subsequently, in back-to-back games against West Catholic and Holland Christian, Sugar matched his point total of 44 points. He accumulated 30 rebounds (19 vs. West Catholic) and 13 assists (7 vs. West Catholic) in both games. Corky Meinecke, sportswriter for *The Grand Rapids Press*, commented, "That's a good season for some players."[9] Sugar had 40- and 39-point games in his second season suiting up for Creston. According to his scrapbook, he would average 33.2 points per game (29.6 in City League games) and shoot a blistering 54 percent, in addition to averaging 6.8 assists and 8.5 rebounds per game.

Former East Grand Rapids' player Dave Jennings describes playing a summer league game against Creston as "a total nightmare."

 As soon as we got on the court, it was like 'Holy smokes!' Melvin's hands were so big that he was whipping this ball around like it was glued to his fingers. We were all in pretty good shape and had played a lot of basketball, but they raced out to like 24-3. We called a timeout in order to figure out what to do with Melvin. We fought really hard to come back against him. We started passing the ball inside more, doing some highs and lows, getting more physical on defense. Then they stepped up their 'D' a little more. You'd come out on Melvin to guard him, then he'd take a step back and shoot it. He must have had 30 points and didn't even break a sweat. He played effortlessly, even though he was working hard. We were playing against a guy with Division 1 talent. It was fun to play against someone like that. Back in the day, we all had pretty big egos, but after playing Melvin in that summer league game, we were much humbler.

Creston's sweet-shooting phenom continued to demonstrate those skills his senior year. In a season-opening thriller over Kalamazoo's Loy Norrix, Sugar scored fifty-one points. His shots slung from all over the floor slayed the Knights 90-89. Art Preuss of *The Grand Rapids Press* highlighted afterward, "The 155-pound senior found himself in a crowd every time he touched the ball, but it didn't stop him from throwing shots up to the hoop from everywhere but the bleachers. On some shots, it looked as though he was doing all he could just to be able to fling the ball that far with one hand."[10]

His performance against the Knights was even more outstanding, given that the Saturday prior to the game, Sugar had sprained his ankle. The previous Sunday morning, Creston's star player was on crutches worshipping at New Hope Baptist Church. The following Friday night, he became a living example of God's healing power at North East Middle School.

Around a month later, on December 20, University of Michigan's head basketball coach, Johnny Orr, drove from Ann Arbor for some last-minute Christmas shopping in Grand Rapids. Only he wasn't looking in a store. Instead, it was in the gymnasium of Grand Rapids Christian where he would see just what his Wolverines needed. Sugar caused Polar Bear fans to shout and Eagles fans to pout. He impressed Orr by popping in 45 points in a 90-77 victory. He went 21-29 from the floor and 3 for 3 from the free throw line. *The Grand Rapids Press* Sports Editor Bob Becker wrote, "The University of Michigan basketball coach was taking a first-hand look at the present he'd most like under his Christmas tree this year...a sweet Melvin Doll. Just wind him up and watch him pump away from anywhere inside 35 feet."[11]

In early February, Sugar arrived late to a home game against Ottawa Hills. That night, he atypically earned most of his thirty points from the charity stripe, going 16 for 19. In the process, however, he managed to make a rare 5-point play after he was fouled in the act of shooting a basket. Ottawa Hill's Coach Jim Weddle expressed his frustration at the ref's call by doing his rendition of the "Muhammad Ali shuffle." Sugar won two more shots at the line.[12]

The Indians' attack didn't necessarily cause Sugar's unexpected lack of firepower. His late arrival prevented him from properly warming up for the game. Bobbie says,

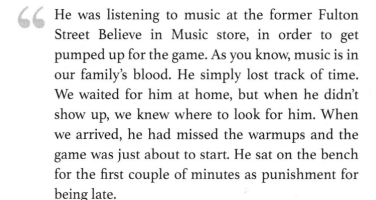

> He was listening to music at the former Fulton Street Believe in Music store, in order to get pumped up for the game. As you know, music is in our family's blood. He simply lost track of time. We waited for him at home, but when he didn't show up, we knew where to look for him. When we arrived, he had missed the warmups and the game was just about to start. He sat on the bench for the first couple of minutes as punishment for being late.

In his 18 years of coaching, Grand Haven's Al Schaffer calls one game a standout. The Buccaneers triumphed over Creston's Polar Bears, 98-96, in 1979. Sugar pumped in 41 points while Grand Haven's Bob Gerris scored 37. Grand Haven's athletic director, Steve Sluka, said it was the greatest high school game he had ever seen.[13] And in one of his last regular season games for the Polar Bears, Sugar marooned the Maroons of Holland Christian, scoring 50 points while going

24-34 from the field for a sizzling hot shooting percentage of 69%.[14]

Throughout his final season for Creston, Sugar averaged over 32 points per game, pulling down an average of 8.3 rebounds, making 5.3 steals, and dishing out 7.8 assists per contest.[15] The two-time Grand Rapids City League scoring champ shot 58 percent from the floor. In four of his most impressive games that year, he exploded the nets for 51, 50, 47, and 41 points.[16]

Sugar's supporting cast his junior and senior seasons wasn't as talented. Still, Creston only lost fourteen games in his three-year career. And he played the majority of those games in the super competitive Grand Rapids City League. When he donned the blue and gold for the Polar Bears, the Grand Rapids City League consisted of seven schools. There were four public schools (Creston, the Ottawa Hills Indians, the Central Rams, and the Union Red Hawks), and three private schools (the Grand Rapids Christian Eagles, the Catholic Central Cougars, and the West Catholic Falcons).

Sugar recalls that when he played, the City League was tough and the entire league was balanced from top to bottom. Every player and team played their hardest, especially when facing him and his fellow Polar Bears. "They charged at me with everything, every night," he says, laughing. "Guys literally hung on my arms to stop me. The whole City League used to be the most physical league in Grand Rapids. They had a different mentality than the players from other leagues. They were taking no prisoners. Everyone was going to bring it."

Coach Haskins agrees. "People don't understand how tough the City League was back then. He was playing against very good teams every night. They were thinking up all kinds of defenses against him. We had to come up with different things to help him. But he just scored."[17]

According to Haskins, "We saw every defensive scheme

imaginable: double teams, triple teams, the triangle in one where he used to go around screens, box in ones, four in ones. At times all five players went after him. But once he got a person to back up a little bit, he would shoot it and score."

Another strategy teams used in an attempt to stop Sugar was to implement a more aggressive playing style. For example, Central High's Coach Tim Clinkscales' Rams were notorious for their harassing defense and physical play. Outside of the city league, the Birmingham Brother Rice Warriors, located about twenty miles northwest of Detroit, also used aggressive physical tactics in an effort to thwart Creston's scoring machine. Led by 6'10" All-American Tim Andree, Coach Bill Norton's Warriors were one of the top-ranked teams in the state. In his junior year, Sugar had embarrassed the visiting Warriors by scoring 40 points in a losing effort, 73-59.

As Scott Scholten of *The Grand Rapids Press* illustrated, "Goliath (Birmingham junior center Tim Andree) lost the battle, but he won the war."[18] In response, when they met again his senior year at Brother Rice's gym, Sugar faced what Haskins describes as "an NBA style of defense" as his defenders would push him on the hip to throw him off balance. Haskins' complaints to the refs were often met with silent whistles, resulting in his star player being held to 23 points, 12 of those from the charity stripe. Creston came out on the losing end, 67-50. Towards the end of the game, however, Sugar satisfactorily silenced the hostile crowd. He hoisted a 40-foot moon shot that hit nothing but net.[19]

Yet, in spite of aggressive opposition, Sugar had only one sprained ankle during his entire three-year career at Creston. Haskins says, "He got hit in the face a couple of times, and once in a while ended up bleeding, but it didn't faze him a bit. He's a tough kid."

Some teams went into a stall to prevent Sugar from piling up points against them. For example, in a game against West

Catholic, Coach Jim Schafer directed his players to take some time off the clock. They didn't attempt a shot for the first five minutes of the game. In his post-game comments, Schafer explained, "We figured the less time we had to play defense on Melvin (McLaughlin) the better it would be for us. So that meant we had to control the ball."[20] Even though the Falcons limited Sugar to 24 points for the game, they couldn't shut him down entirely. In the third quarter, he exploded for seven field goals and two free throws, leading the Polar Bears to a 75-52 victory.

While the City League teams and traditional opponents of Creston were familiar with Sugar's shooting range, a lot of other teams were caught off guard when he pulled up from just anywhere on the floor. By the time they tried to guard him, it was too late. No matter what defensive schemes teams devised in order to stop him, he overcame them by just going further and further out. He lulled the opposition into thinking that they didn't have to guard him from that far out, making his feats even more astonishing.

Even teams familiar with his range couldn't stop him. Everywhere he played, Sugar launched his on-target bombs that exploded into nothing but net. Union's Todd Stacey recalls battling against Sugar and his sloth of Polar Bears. Red Hawks' standouts Carl Roscoe and Charlie Brown would join him in the fray. Stacey says,

 We had great games. I was a pretty good defender. But he could just pull up from anywhere. One time he hit me up from the hash mark after just crossing over half court. He was just picking me apart. I was shattered. It wasn't like he's going to shoot 20% against you in a night. He would eventually go off. You may stop him a little bit for a quarter, but eventually you knew it was like the rain coming. If you could keep him under forty that was probably a decent day.

Grand Rapids Christian's coach, the late Ken Zandee, revealed that he knew Sugar was going to get his points, so his main goal was stopping the rest of the team. Though Zandee boasted that his Eagles played more of a team game, he also acknowledged that Sugar was a once-in-a-lifetime kind of player. When Zandee coached at Christian, he relied on the "Wheel Offense," working the ball inside for higher percentage shots. Consequently, he admitted, "I'm glad I didn't coach when they had the three-point play, especially when we played against Melvin."

His body frame often fooled opponents, who reasoned that he wasn't all that strong. Time and again Sugar proved to be more durable than meets the eye. The epitome of a pure shooter, he could shoot it from anywhere, anytime, and make it. Everyone else was simply at his mercy game after game.

When Sugar played in high school, the courts had short dashes known as "hash marks" perpendicular to the sidelines, around 25 feet from the basket. Generally, Haskins cleared Sugar to shoot from the hash marks on in, for he had no problems making his shots from that distance. Then again, for Sugar to hit from forty feet wasn't unusual. It was customary.

During Sugar's tenure at Creston, Don Edwards was his gym teacher. He taught Sugar how to shoot off the glass or backboard. Hence, "the banks were open" on Tuesday and Friday nights in Grand Rapids. Opponents learned to beware when the Creston Polar Bears prowled the playing floors during the basketball seasons from 1976-1979.

Even though long-distance shooting was his forte, Sugar wasn't a one-trick-pony when it came to putting the ball in the hoop. His quickness allowed him to easily penetrate past his slower-footed defenders and inside for lay-ups, making him a double threat to guard. Haskins still recalls a spectacular shot over Brother Rice's 6'10" All-American Tim Andree. Andree went on to play for Notre Dame University.

> We had an out-of-bounds play we practiced over and over. Melvin was supposed to get the inbounds pass or get it back to the guy coming back in from out of bounds. In one game, he cut towards underneath the basket around a screen. We had picked him to get the ball and square up and let it fly from what would have been a three-point play. But instead, when he made that cut to the basket, he made a hook shot over Tim Andree.

Haskins is emphatic: Sugar was an all-around great player:

> Not only was he an outstanding shooter, but he was a passer. He could see the floor and he could play great 'D'. He wasn't a big kid in high school, but he could shoot it from all over the place. He could drive it to the hole and shoot from the outside. He had a lot of skills people had never seen. His range was unbelievable.[21]

Moreover, Haskins says, "He would have shattered all scoring records with the three-pointer. In high school, he would have averaged over 40 points per game. He averaged 30-some points a game without the three-point shot. His shots were well beyond three-point range."

Unfortunately, the films of Sugar's playing days at Creston disappeared over the years. Hence, Sugar's high school games, for the most part, live on only in the memories of those who were privileged to watch him play. And those make for some sweet memories, indeed.

13

SWEET MEMORIES OF A SHINING STAR

 Heroes come and go, but legends are forever.

— KOBE BRYANT

Creston High School closed in 2016. Though reels of Sugar's games may be lost, the legacy of the Polar Bears' sweet-shooting alumnus is in no danger of becoming extinct. He left behind more than sweet memories with the coaches and players. A highlight film of moves and shots are permanently embedded in the hearts and minds of those who saw him play in high school. Those who witnessed his games cannot help but pass on to the next generation their personal testimonies of what they saw and experienced. For stories to outlive the generations that experienced them testifies to the power of their stories.

Concerning the life of Jesus, the beloved disciple John supposed that if all the many other things he did were written down, the whole world would not have room for the books that would be written (see John 21:25). Instead, the purpose of his

Gospel was that his readers would believe that Jesus is the promised Messiah (John 20:31).

Similarly, there are so many other Sugar stories that this chapter and the rest of this book don't have enough pages to cover. The following high school memories are written, that the readers who didn't see him play may be convinced that he was the real deal. More than that, to experience the possibility of the power of a natural gift, hard work, and a dream.

In my own case, I first saw Sugar play at Aquinas College, where Catholic Central hosted Creston. I was a freshman in high school. This was his senior year. I didn't even remember the final score of the game or who won, but *The Grand Rapids Press* dates the game on January 5, 1979. Sugar scored 14 fourth-quarter points in leading the Polar Bears over the Cougars, 78-64. This win secured their first place in the City League at 5-1. The box score shows him with sixteen field goals and two free throws for a total of thirty-four points for the night.[1]

What I do remember, however, is the unexplainable joy I felt watching Sugar play. The gym's atmosphere could be compared to a rock concert where he was the leading singer, or to a big party with Sugar the guest of honor. He was like a preacher at a revival meeting. He either inspired his current converts even further by his play, or else made new converts of those who had never seen him play before.

From the start, I was at the edge of my seat. Even in the pre-game warm-up, Sugar led his teammates on the court with a finger roll lay-up over the rim. To add to the party-like atmosphere, The Earth, Wind and Fire song, "Shining Star" played in the background while players loosened up. Sugar was definitely the shining star that night, shining bright for everyone in the gym to see. Throughout the game, it seemed as if every shot he took and made was beyond the hash mark. The moment he crossed the mid court line, people from both sides of the stands cried out, "Shoot it, Sugar!" More often than not, he answered by launching baskets from an audacious range. I witnessed a God-given talent that I had never seen before. Nor have I seen the likes since, though I have played with, worked with and coached a lot of talented players over the years.

But more than sheer talent stood out that night. Something about his character and demeanor was exceptional, as well. Ever since, I've been a devoted Sugar fan. Not only for the way he performed on the court, but the way he has conducted himself on and off the court.

Bob Becker, former *Grand Rapids Press* sports editor, first saw Sugar play as a sophomore. His impression was similar to mine.

 Everyone was telling me, "You got go see this kid play ball!" So, I walk into the gym and watch Melvin simply light it up. After the game, I went to talk to him, and when he came out of the locker room, there must have been nine little girls around him, I'm talking about 11-year olds, 13-year olds, screaming, "Oh, Melvin! Oh, Melvin!" He was like the Pied Piper, and he was smiling at everybody. When I got a chance to interview him, he was the nicest kid you could ever hope to see. I knew that he had a future ahead of him. Not only could he shoot like nobody I've ever seen, but he just liked people and people liked him. If Melvin walked into your room, he'd be your friend in three minutes. Back at the office, I said, "I know he's a great basketball player, but that kid is really something else. He can just reach out to anybody." From that point on every time I saw him, it was the same deal: Sugar with a bunch of girls, Sugar who could just light it up, and Sugar with a big smile.

Becker adds,

 His biggest problem at Creston was he really didn't have a 6'11" stud in the middle, someone he could build around. If he had someone who would force the other team to guard the middle, so the outside was open, but the way they were... They had some good players, but teams just tried to shut down Sugar, because they didn't have a Matt Steigenga to guard with him. I wonder what numbers he'd have with the three-point line both in high school and college. He had great numbers anyway, but he didn't score many lay-ups. A lay-up for him was four steps beyond the mid court line.

Sugar's coach, Jim Haskins, had taken him to Camp Geneva in Holland, Michigan the summer prior to his senior year. He was so impressive that when Creston played against Holland Christian that season, a group of kids who saw him at the camp greeted them at the game. Haskins says, "When we got there all these kids that went to Camp Geneva came to the game. Outside our locker room, we had a huge 'Sugar fan club' all over the place. Of course, he had 50 points, and after the game they circled around him to sign autographs. We couldn't get out of there for another 35-40 minutes. He was still in uniform."

Anthony Gordon, who went on to become a stand-out player at East Kentwood (1988), would eventually play with Sugar on his All-Star team. But his first sight of Sugar came in fourth grade. Gordon's older brother said, "I'm going to take you to see one of the greatest high school basketball players ever." Gordon says,

 It was Melvin's senior year, and the district finals at East Kentwood. It was standing room only. I

was big for my age, and thought I was all that, but I was humbled by what I saw. I couldn't believe where he shot from! My brother said, "You're not going to believe how big his hands are." I'm like, "Really? He's not that tall." But sure enough, he's got really big hands, kind of like Dr. J and Connie Hawkins had in the way they could palm the ball. He knew just how to control the ball.

John Klunder was a couple of grades behind Melvin at Union (1981). After playing in the Junior Varsity game, he watched Sugar's Polar Bears play his Red Hawks.

 I can't imagine trying to guard him. It had to be embarrassing in front of so many people to try to guard Sugar. I'm glad I never got the chance! We could not wait until our JV game was over so we could watch Mel play. Union's varsity won the league that year, splitting with Creston. Mel had 33 and 39 against our varsity. Todd Stacy was supposedly our defensive stopper but nobody stopped Mel. I never saw a guy shoot so well and consistent from so far out. The opening tip always seemed to end up in his hands way out by the hash mark, and he jacked it up immediately and swished it. The game's two seconds old, Mel already nailed a bomb, and the crowd's going crazy. Greatest shooter I ever saw.

Klunder's classmate, Linda Chandler, began dating Sugar before seeing him play. Her first game was Creston against the Red Hawks.

> When I first met him, I was cheering for the JV, but I stuck around for the Varsity game because I knew Melvin. Bennette Gay's mom sat on Union's side and screamed "Shoot it!" as soon as Melvin got the ball. He shoots from half court and it goes in. She and her friends are standing up on our side of the bleachers, saying, "I told you. Don't mess with him! I told you. Can't mess with him!" I thought, "They're on the wrong side." I knew who she was and that Bennette and Melvin were friends. But it was so funny, because she's on our side with her group of friends. They're all standing up when Melvin passed half court, shouting, "Shoot!" At half-time, I don't remember if it counted or not, but he shot the ball from half court and it went in. She and her friends said, "You know I told you so!" They kept it up the whole game.

Pastor Dave Spoelma of Calvin Church in Holland, Michigan remembers the impression Sugar made on him as a middle schooler. His dad brought him to a Grand Haven vs. Creston game.

> My father told me that someone on Creston was really amazing and he wanted to take me to the game. I saw one game and for the rest of my life I have told people this was the best high school basketball player I have ever seen. Melvin would take a step or two over the half court and do a jump shot, not a set shot, and just drain it. He dropped these long-range bombs over and over. The first time Melvin shot from that distance I looked to see if time was running out. Why else

would someone shoot from that distance? I quickly learned that this is what Melvin did. He opened up the defense, so that they had to come out and guard him, which freed up the middle to make Creston a very good basketball team.

Creston alumnus Dave Van Dyke recalls attending the games of Grand Rapids' all-time greatest basketball player. "Watching Melvin McLaughlin, especially his early years, fans (both sides at times) would start chanting 'Shoot' as soon as he crossed half court. Often, he did; almost as often, it was yet another score!"[2] Jerry Hendrick (Creston, 1982) watched many high school legends play, including Glen Rice, Roy Marble, Jalen Rose, Antoine Joubert, Chris Webber. "But," he says,

 I have never seen a better offensive player than Mel. It was great fun watching him pull up from 30 feet out and barely touch the net. I think opposing teams resigned themselves to let him get his 30 points and hoped they could stop everyone else on the team from adding to that total. Too bad he didn't have the three-point line back then.[3]

Sugar's nephew Quinn remembers hanging out after games when he was younger. He waited impatiently for his Uncle Mel to sign autographs for his adoring fans before finally going home. At times, Quinn's father, Bobbie, had his own reasons for being miffed at his brother. Occasionally, Sugar would break into his room. And not just to listen to his records and tapes. He would also help himself to his older brother's more stylish shirts to wear after games. Above all, though, Bobbie recalls people's reaction when watching his brother play.

In the crowd, I overheard comments from people who didn't know he was my brother. "How on earth?" "Oh, my word, did you just see that?" I mean they would be all over him—two or three guys. Box in one, four on one, all coming after him. They didn't realize his range for a long time. He could pull up before you could get to him. By the time they got out there to guard him it would be too late. Whatever they designed for him, he would just go further and further at such a distance. They would think, "Nobody's going to shoot out there, so I don't have to guard him." Mistake! That made him even more incredible. Because of his size, they thought he wasn't all that physical. He was much more durable than meets the eye, because he was a pure scorer. Everybody else was at his mercy.

Alan Whitt, in a column for *The Grand Rapids Press*, gave tribute to the ending of Sugar's high school career.

 When McLaughlin goes, the city will lose about as much as Creston will. For the second year in a row, McLaughlin is this area's only sure-fire All-Stater. No one carries as much impact before, during or after a game as McLaughlin. After he pops in that last 35-footer for the Polar Bears it will mark the end of an era. There will be no more fans to come up to statisticians and reporters to ask for progress reports on McLaughlin's scoring. No longer will there be hordes of high school girls standing outside Northeast Junior High after games asking, "Has Melvin left yet?" No more debates on whether Melvin would have been better off playing for a team where he would average less points, but learn more about other phases of the game. No more Johnny Orr, the basketball coach at Michigan, to come to games and leave after labeling McLaughlin an "offensive wizard."

Whitt continues,

 Those days are over. Some say Melvin is not as good as his scoring stats indicate because he was a member of just one City League championship team (as a tenth grader) during his exciting career, and hardly played then. But he gave a whole lot more to Grand Rapids. People either like him or dislike him, overrate him or underrate him, but there was never a question he could shoot that basketball.[4]

Though his playing days at Creston are long over, Sugar made a lasting impression on those privileged to watch him light it up for the Polar Bears. In 2016 he was selected by MLive.com as the greatest high school player ever to come out of West Michigan.

Over forty years after he shined like a star for all to see, random strangers still walk up to Sugar. They thank him for his inspiration on the court and the sweet memories they still have of him. He did more than shoot a ball. He brought an entire city to its feet in cheers, inspiring generations of people to shoot their best shots.

Mr. and Mrs. Bobbie and Mary Ruth McLaughlin, Sr; Ann Arbor, MI.
Photo courtesy of Bobbie McLaughlin, Jr.

L to R: Melvin, Patricia Veronica (sister), Mary Ruth McLaughlin
(mother), Grand Rapids, at Patricia's wedding. Photo courtesy of Bobbie
McLaughlin, Jr.

McLaughlin Family Reunion, Ann Arbor, Christmas Day. Photo courtesy of Bobbie McLaughlin, Jr.

Sugar and the undefeated 1974-1975 Iroquois Braves, 7th Grade Team, Iroquois Middle School, Grand Rapids, MI. Photo courtesy of Mel Atkins.

Super Soph Team 1976-77 Creston High School Polar Bears, Grand Rapids; 24-2, Class A Quarter-Finalists. Photo courtesy of Bobbie McLaughlin, Jr.

Sugar's underhand lay-up for Creston High. Mlive Media Group, all rights reserved. Used with permission. Photographer: Anne Moore Butzner.

Sugar launches for two of 40 points against Birmingham Brother Rice, December 1977. Mlive Media Group. All rights reserved. Used with permission. Photographer: Rex D. Larson.

Sugar is all smiles after signing with Central Michigan, Creston High Auditorium, April 17, 1979. Mlive Media Group Press Photo. All rights reserved. Used with permission.

Melvin "Sugar" McLaughlin had a touch of sweetness Saturday afternoon as the CMU men's basketball team defeated Ball State, 84-83. The Grand Rapids sophomore launches the winning basket with time running out.

Sugar's 40-foot buzzer beater vs. Ball State, Rose Arena,
March 2, 1981. (Central Michigan Life photo archives,
March 2, 1981, courtesy of the Clarke Historical Library.)

Sugar swishes a free throw, 1982. Photo by Robert Barclay,
courtesy of the Clarke Historical Library.

Don't miss additional photos and footage at
SweetShotBasketballCamp.com TwigAllAmerican.com !

*Sugar shakes off a clutter of Ohio University Bobcats, 1982. Photo by
Robert Barclay, courtesy of the Clarke Historical Library.*

*Sugar splits two Western Michigan University Broncos for a lay-up, 1983.
Photo by Robert Barclay, courtesy of the Clarke Historical Library.*

Sugar's Poster Shot adorned many Central Michigan dorm rooms, 1983.
Photo by Robert Barclay, courtesy of the Clarke Historical Library.

SUGAR

From the school that gave the NBA Dan Roundfield, James McElroy and Ben Poquette comes Melvin "Sugar" McLaughlin, one of the sweetest of them all, Central Michigan University's scoring machine.

Named the Most Valuable Player in the Mid-American Conference a year ago after averaging 23.2 points a game, the 6-foot-1, 165-pound senior guard is a legitimate All-American candidate. "Sugar" is a pure shooter, a team leader and excellent ball-handler. He is called "CMU's next professional" by his coach, Dick Parfitt.

Central Michigan University

MELVIN **SUGAR** McLAUGHLIN

Central Michigan's All-American Candidate "Sugar Packet Promotion."
Photo of packet courtesy of Bobbie McLaughlin, Jr.

Background photo from the Gus Macker Hall of Fame: Sugar on the main court of the Gus Macker Tournament, Belding, Michigan. L-R: Sugar, Scott McNeal, and Bobbie.

*Sugar, Vern, "Little Sugar," and Bobbie attend the 45th
Anniversary of the Gus Macker 3 on 3 Tournament in
Belding, MI.*

*L to R, Charles Tucker, Magic Johnson, George Gervin,
unidentified coach, Kevin Loder, Derek Harper, Sugar,
Daryl Dawkins, 1983. Photo courtesy of Bobbie
McLaughlin, Jr.*

Bennette Gay (L) inspired Sugar to begin his own basketball camp. Dave Ginsberg (R). Photo courtesy Johnny Lui, 2018.

1993 Chippewa Athletic Hall of Fame Inductees, Sugar and sports broadcaster Dick Enberg, 1993. Photo courtesy of Bobbie McLaughlin, Jr.

Sugar (aka "Radar"), Reggie Theus, and Magic Johnson, Lakers' LA Forum, 1994. Photo courtesy of Bobbie McLaughlin, Jr.

Central Michigan University retires Sugar's #14 jersey,
1999. Photo by Robert Barclay, courtesy of the Clarke
Historical Library.

Sugar and his mentor, the late Don "The Animal" Edwards,
April 2005. Photo by Lance Wynn/The Grand Rapids Press.
Mlive Media Group. All rights reserved. Used with permission.

Sugar and his Sweet Shot campers, East Kentwood High School, August,
2018. Photo courtesy of Brian Gilmore.

Award Ceremony for Grand Rapids' Greatest All-Time Player, and his high school coach, Jim Haskins, 2016. Photo courtesy of Anthony Gordon.

Vern and Sugar, Global Christianity and Sports Conference, Calvin College, 2019. Photo courtesy of Kathryn Wendt-Mackey.

Strategizing for greatness. Sugar and nephew Quinn Adams, East Kentwood High, August 2019. Photo courtesy of Henry Schutte, <photoshooty.com>

"Dare to be great!" Sugar's Sweet Shot campers at East Kentwood High School, August, 2019. Photo courtesy of Henry Schutte <photoshooty.com>

Coach Dave Ginsberg and his prized recruit reunite. Photo courtesy of Bobbie McLaughlin, Jr.

Author Vern Wendt shares Sugar's secret of success, East Kentwood High School, August 2019. Photo courtesy of Henry Schutte <photoshooty.com>

Sugar enjoys a "taste of heaven" at King Park, August 2019. Photo courtesy of Henry Schutte <photoshooty.com>

Vern, Sugar, Little Sugar, and Bobbie, in front of the McLaughlin family home on Prince Street, August 2019. Photo courtesy of Henry Schutte <photoshooty.com>

Vern, Sugar, and Bobbie at Sugar Mel's Sweet Shot Basketball Camp, August 2019. Photo courtesy of Eli Kaminski. Used with permission.

Sugar shoots at King Park, August 2019. Make sure your team has your back! Photo courtesy of Henry Schutte <photoshooty.com>

15

CAN ANY GOOD BASKETBALL PLAYER COME OUT OF GRAND RAPIDS?

 "Nazareth! Can anything good come from there?"
Nathanael asked.
> "Come and see," said Philip.

— JOHN 1:46

I n the late 1970s, AAU basketball teams, traveling squads, and social media didn't exist. Players from smaller markets had to overcome the biases of the major media markets. When Sugar played for Grand Rapids Creston, the *Detroit Free Press* and the *Detroit News* tended to promote the players in Michigan from the east side of state. As a result, he wasn't given the recognition he deserved outside of Grand Rapids. Instead, he had to prove that he was an exception to numerous presumptions.

Style of play. Sugar faced all kinds of aggressive opposition to stop him from single-handedly dominating the game, especially in the Grand Rapids City League. However, a common perception was that players and teams were more physical on

144 | REV. DR. VERNON E. WENDT, JR.

the east side of the state. Scouts deemed those players as more thoroughly prepared for the rigors of collegiate competition.

Prejudice of Scouts. Because of their reputations, the scouts tended to focus on players from the Detroit, Saginaw, and Flint areas. The rest of the state's players were considered high risk and not worth their time and energy. According to one anonymous athletic director, "Scouts only have a certain amount of time, and they put it to use in places where they think it will be most productive. Grand Rapids players who are not recruited might beat the pants off the other kids who are. But we don't have the reputation."[1]

School's Lack of Powerhouse Reputation. Ottawa Hills won back-to-back state championships in 1968 and 1969. Still, Saginaw, Flint Northern, and some of the Detroit area schools roll out prospects like Ford rolls out cars. Grand Rapids has no history of producing such a lineup.

The Character of Grand Rapids. Like any city, there are some rough parts. Overall, though, Grand Rapids is a relatively safe place to live, especially compared to cities of similar size. In contrast, Detroit, Flint and Saginaw consistently rank among the top most violent cities in the country annually. A player's tenacity on the court is assumed to match the perceived character of the city they're from. Scott Scholten writes, "Grand Rapids was an All-American city which teaches All-American values. The killer instinct so vital to success in major college athletics isn't necessarily a byproduct of our climate." As one area coach characterized, "To play at a major school, you've got to eat raw meat. Our kids are too nice."[2]

Nonetheless, in spite of any biases, the Detroit media couldn't overlook a player as gifted as Sugar. Sugar made the second team Class A All-State team his junior year and the first team Class A All-State team in his senior year. Notably absent from both the Class A and Class B All-State teams in both years, however, were the rest of the players from the Grand Rapids City League.

In addition, Sugar was the only player on the state's west side to make the Michigan All-Star team his senior year. Joining him were fellow first team Class A All-State members Marlow McClain from Detroit Murray-Wright, Erich Santifer from Ann Arbor Huron, Tim Andree from Birmingham Brother Rice, and James Koger from Saginaw High School. In addition, Dereck Perry, from Class B's Detroit River Rouge, was considered one of the top college prospects in the state.

When playing with the Michigan High School All-Stars, Sugar awed his teammates, opponents, fans, and the media alike. Post position teammates, Tim Andree and 6'6" Derrick Perry, opened up the perimeter, and further accentuated his shooting range. The *Detroit Free Press* described a Michigan High School All-Stars win over a Yugoslavian national team: "The Friday night game at Schoolcraft Community College was over in a matter of minutes. Six-foot-10 Tim Andree of Birmingham Brother Rice opened things up for the perimeter players, and then Melvin McLaughlin of Grand Rapids Creston, began hitting his jumpers from downtown Livonia."[3]

With a more talented cast, Sugar proved that he was more than a one-dimensional player, shining as a playmaker and defensive stopper. In a game against Washington DC's best prep players, he held Deago McCoy, rated in the top 20 players in the country, to just four points.[4] His deft passing skills helped lead the Michigan All-Stars to the finals of the All-American Cage Classic. They eventually lost to favored Val-Pack Novak. The winners were led by Ohio's 6-foot-8 All-American Clark Kellogg, with 26 points. Six-foot-6 All-Stater Colin Irish added 22 points. Sugar was the shooting star for the losing Michigan All-Stars with 22 points.[5]

He was so outstanding in the All-American Cage Classic that UNLV coach Jerry Tarkanian could hardly contain himself.

Bobbie says, "He found me at half-time saying, 'Your brother is amazing! I came here looking for a big man, but I've found what I'm looking for!'" Tarkanian aggressively recruited Sugar to play for his Runnin' Rebels throughout the tournament. After a game against the DC All Stars, Michigan All Star coach Carl Smith shared, "I had to chase Tarkanian away from (Melvin) today so that he could get some rest."[6]

In a major media market, Sugar would have been heralded as one of the top players in his class. But in spite of stellar statistics, since he came out of Grand Rapids, people assumed his competition to be inferior. Not only did he face the bias of the Detroit media locally, but nationally he experienced biases of the other major markets, such as Chicago, Los Angeles, and New York.

Given today's AAU, Traveling Teams, and various basketball camps featuring the top prospects in the country, players are constantly competing against each other. Consequently, they can be easily evaluated by the scouts. More often than not, the elite have been competing against each other since middle school, and have teamed up with each other at a camp or on an all-star team.

In addition, today's world consists of 24-hour sports cable networks, smartphone videos, twitter accounts, blogs, and social media. It really doesn't matter where you come from. Instead, it's how well you market yourself.

But in the late 1970s, the best prep players were often limited to camps. There, they competed against each other to claim to be the best high school players in the country. These all-star camps greatly reduced the time and expense of college recruiting. Rather than traveling icy winter roads to remote high school gyms, college coaches viewed the nation's best prospects at a central location. Intense competition gave coaches a unique opportunity to see if a prospect could hold his own against players of comparable size and talent. Theoretically, a good showing at a big all-star camp could vault a player from the middle of nowhere into national recognition.

Three top summer basketball camps in the country existed when Sugar played in high school. Howard Garfinkel's 5-Star Camp in Pittsburgh; Bill Cronhaur's BC camp in Milledgeville, Georgia; and Sportsworld's Superstar Invitational Basketball Camp in Santa Barbara, California. The BC and Sportsworld camps sought to attract the best players with invitations, but 5-Star relied on its reputation to draw the top prospects.

The summer prior to his senior year, Sugar received an exclusive invitation to the BC Camp. The original camp directors, Bill Bolton and Bill Cronhauer, founded the camp in 1977 and named it after Cronhauer's initials, B.C. At the time, Bolton was an assistant at Florida State University, and one of the premier recruiters in college basketball. Cronhauer was a sportswriter for the *St. Petersburg Times*, as well as the editor for *B/C Scouting Services,* "America's foremost recruiting publication."[7]

In its sixteen-year history from 1977-1992, the BC Camp was recognized as the premier basketball camp in the country.[8] The first year of the camp ran only one session. Of its 160 players, eighteen went on to play in the NBA.[9] The following summer of 1978, when Sugar attended the camp, however, is considered to have the most talented players of all its years. The 1978 camp promotional poster boasted an attractive brunette with a winsome smile, by the name of Vanna White. Bolton, in an effort to spice up the camp a bit, picked Vanna out of around 100 pictures at an Atlanta modeling agency.[10]

However, Sugar's wheel of fortune at the camp would prove to be a harbinger of things to come. He experienced for the first time the unexpected politics of the game he loved. Given his performance that week compared to his second-tiered rating afterward, the selection panel appeared to be clueless. Or else they needed to buy some vowels when it came to choosing the names of the top players to make the first All-Star team.

That summer especially, much fanfare surrounded the BC Camp. Premier players would attend, many ranked as preseason All-Americans. The graduating class of 1978-1979 is considered the most talented class in high school basketball history. Bob Gibbons was recognized as the top-rated high school talent evaluator in the country. His top five players in this class were Ralph Samson, Clark Kellogg, Sam Bowie, James Worthy and Isiah Thomas. But even in Isiah's hometown of Chicago, some scouts had ranked Bloom High School's Raymond McCoy ahead of Thomas. Consequently, Isiah turned down his invitation to the BC camp and chose to attend 5-Star that summer.

Sugar and the other Michigan invitees piled into Birmingham Brother Rice's Coach Bill Norton's station wagon. They made their way down to Georgia from Michigan. Sugar would play against the top-rated high school players that he had read about in the scouting magazines. He was eager to see how he compared. That summer BC Camp held two sessions, June 11-17 and August 6-12. Not all the players were there when Sugar attended. Regardless, Sugar recalls, "I was looking forward to playing and seeing how good those guys really were."

According to the camp's history, when Sugar attended their June 1978 session:

- 215 players attended from 33 different states.
- Sixty of the campers were 6'6" or taller. 7'4" Ralph Sampson from Harrisburg, Virginia was the tallest.
- 6'8" Antoine Carr from Wichita, Kansas was the camp MVP, dominating everyone he faced. His cross-town rival, 6'3½" Ricky Ross, won the Top 20 All Star Game MVP as the leading scorer with 22 points.

- Sugar's Michigan All-Star teammate, 6'10" Tim Andree, of Birmingham Brother Rice, won the week's Mr. Hustle award and 6'1" Jimmy Gray of Louisville Durrett, Kentucky, won the slam-dunk competition.
- James Banks of Atlanta Smith, Georgia was selected the most promising junior player. Clyde Corley, 6'4", of Pontiac Central, Michigan and 6'7" Kevin Darmody of Bishop O' Connor in Springfield, Virginia were the MVPs of the second and third top 20 All Star Games, respectively.
- Among the guards who reportedly stood out that week were Ross; Quintin Dailey of Baltimore, Maryland; and Jimmy Gray. Point guards included Jimmy Braddock of Chattanooga's Baylor School and John Paxson of Kettering Altar, Ohio.
- In addition, 210 college coaches were in attendance, and several of the top 20 programs had their entire staff on hand. According to one of the top five program coaches, eighty of the players that attended that week could have contributed on their level.[11]

Glaringly missing in these highlights, however, is an unheralded 6-foot, 155-pound guard from Grand Rapids, Michigan by the name of Melvin McLaughlin. As leading scorer, Sugar averaged over 44 points per game. He also led his team to winning the championship that week. Sugar reminisces with his infectious smile and a gleam in his eyes.

We got ready for team play where I was mixed in with other invited players. Right away I began to establish myself as the go-to guy in the first game. We were playing against some guys from the first team preseason All-American teams, and I went right through them. I destroyed them. After the game, the highly ranked players we played against or were watching, were in shock, saying, "Great game! I can't believe you can shoot like that! How did you learn how to do that?" I thought, "Wow! This guy was the pre-season top player in the nation and I just obliterated him." That confirmed that I belonged there.

For the rest of the week, Sugar dominated not only the top players in his class but some of the top players in the history of basketball. The players who witnessed him play all week kept affirming him, "You got it! You've got to be in the first team All Star Game."

Searching the names of the first team All-Stars posted outside of the locker room, he couldn't find his name listed anywhere. Rather, he saw John Paxon's name, whose brother Jim had starred for Dayton and was playing at the time for the NBA's Portland Trail Blazers. He saw guards Daily, Gray, and Braddock. Sugar checked again. Maybe his eyes tricked him. "There must be a mistake!" He finally discovered his name among the players on the second team All-Stars.

Other players noticing the slight came to him in disbelief. "It's not fair! How is that possible? There's no way you should be in the second All-Star game." Sugar reflects, "I couldn't believe it! I totally lost my respect for the people in charge there. In protest, I went back to my dorm and didn't play."

Saginaw High School coach Charlie Coles learned about his boycott and tried to persuade him to play. "We understand your situation. You definitely belong in the first All-Star game, but you need to still play. We know how you feel, but if doesn't look good to the college coaches if you refuse to play."

Sugar refused to budge. "I just proved to all those cats that I'm a better player than all these characters and deserve to be on the first team. I have to stand up for what is right. Because you know it's a bunch of bull! And everyone else does as well." Consequently, the BC website implies that Sugar scored zero points, while playing for the second team All-Stars.[12]

The camp advertised itself as a place to help relatively unknown players get exposure. But when an unheralded player from Grand Rapids outperformed their highly ranked preseason All-Americans, their ad turned out to be fake news.

"They wanted to promote the All-Americans at their camp. They didn't want to acknowledge that my team and I defeated everybody," Sugar says now. "If you look at my college career and compare statistics, I had a better career individually than most all of those guys."

When Sugar returned from the camp, Dave Ginsberg heard from some coaches who were there, and tried to console his star recruit. "I heard you got screwed down there. I'm really sorry about that. But, do you know what they wrote about you? Great shooter, great ball handler, but bad attitude!"

Jimmy Boylen, learning of Sugar's experience at the camp, knew how the high school All-Star camps tend to work. He said, "That doesn't surprise me one bit. Reputation is everything. So, a guy goes to a camp and loses his reputation, they aren't going back again. Consequently, their coaches aren't going to send the next guy. A lot of the players are rated already when they get there, whether they play good or not."

Unfortunately, the camp didn't begin filming until several years later. We can only envision that summer of 1978 in Milledgeville, Georgia. One week, when Sugar shone brighter than all the other stars, while draining shots from all over the court.

16

LOYALTY WINS SUGAR FOR THE CHIPPEWAS

66 Oh, the places you'll go! There is fun to be done.
There are points to be scored. There are games to
be won. And the magical things you can do with
the ball will make you the winning-est winner
of all.

— THEODORE SEUSS GEISEL (AKA DR. SEUSS)

When Bobbie promised to see to his little brother's
education, he was determined to keep his
commitment to his mother, though at the time he
didn't know how he was going to possibly fulfill it. But seeing
Melvin excel on the hardwood, he realized that Sugar might
just get a college scholarship for basketball. However, his dad
was realistic about the idea of his youngest child going to
college. "It isn't necessary, and we can't afford it."

Bobbie countered his dad's skepticism. "Dad, he's playing
basketball, really, really well. He can get a scholarship."

"That's what it will have to be. We certainly don't have the
means to pay for him to go to college by ourselves!" When

Sugar made the varsity basketball team at Creston as a sophomore, Bobbie was convinced that his brother could receive a full-ride scholarship. "I could see what he was doing in the games. But I also saw people's reaction in the stands, in awe at everything he did. They saw what I saw. I was really happy that it wasn't just me, and I was certain he was going to go to college."

By 1979, Sugar's senior year, scouts from all over the country attended his games to see him in action. Over two hundred colleges offered him scholarships. Coach Haskins had a student aid working for him to keep track of the colleges that interested his star player. At Melvin's thumbs-up or thumbs-down, according to Haskins, "The aid gave him three schools to consider at a time. Once he got done considering those three, he was given three more. But he wasn't allowed to consider any more until he had first considered the three schools he was given."

Collectively, three shopping bags burst with recruiting letters addressed to Sugar. The letters came from schools all over the country, especially the Midwest. The decision would not be easy.

All the Division I coaches in Michigan courted him. Michigan's Johnny Orr and Michigan State's Jud Heathcote were at the helm of the state's two Big Ten schools. Michigan had long been considered the school to attend by elite players in the state. Originally from Ann Arbor, Sugar had a special affinity for the Wolverines. On the other hand, Gregory Kelser and Magic Johnson had just led Michigan State to a second consecutive Big Ten title. And in a game that would draw the highest television ratings in college basketball history, they teamed up to help the Spartans capture their first NCAA Championship over Larry Bird's Indiana State Sycamores.

The University of Detroit made the first round of the NCAA tournament that year and a few years earlier, had made the

Sweet Sixteen. Willie McCarter, newly hired at the University of Detroit, replaced David "Smokey" Gaines. He picked up where Smokey left off, trying to lure Sugar. If he suited up for the Titans, he predicted, Sugar could be the next Terry Deurod.[1]

Central Michigan, the top team in the MAC Conference, had played in the 1979 National Invitational Tournament. That team included Grand Rapids' natives Val Bracey and Leon Guydon. Plus, David Ginsberg, assistant coach for Central Michigan, had been attending Sugar's games for years. Eastern Michigan and Western Michigan also urged him to stay in Michigan and play for them.

Additional Big Ten schools especially interested in Sugar's talents were Wisconsin and Minnesota. Bill Cofield, the coach of Wisconsin, was the first black head coach of a major sport in the Big Ten Conference. His squad included future NBA players Wes Matthews and Claude Gregory. Jim Dutcher, Minnesota's head coach, asked Mychal Thompson to convince Sugar to play for his Gophers. Thompson had played under Dutcher in Minneapolis and was the 1978 NBA draft's number one pick. He eventually became the father of Klay Thompson, the outstanding shooter for the Golden State Warriors. In addition, Coach Dutcher sought to entice Sugar to join returning sophomore and eventual NBA player Trent Tucker in the backcourt, along with returning senior forward and future NBA Hall of Famer, Kevin McHale. Also, as a Gopher, he would join 7'3" All-American center, Randy Breuer as incoming freshmen.

Other Midwestern schools sought Sugar, including Cincinnati, Marquette, Notre Dame, and DePaul. Coach Ed Badger of the University of Cincinnati had an outstanding resumé as a former coach of back-to-back undefeated and number one ranked junior college teams at Wright College in Chicago. Badger had a winning record as former head coach of the NBA Chicago Bulls from 1976-1978. However, Cincinnati was already on probation due to recruiting violations. On top of that, they offered employment to Sugar's family members in exchange for his signing with the Bearcats. His dad found this clear violation of NCAA rules unacceptable.

Marquette's head coach Hank Raymonds also had an impressive resumé. Prior to coming to Marquette, he led teams to high school and NAIA Championships. Two years earlier, he had assisted legendary coach Al McGuire with Marquette's 1977-1978 National Championship Team, where he was recognized as the main strategist and organizer of the Warrior's attack. After Raymond succeeded McGuire as head coach, the teams would go on to reach the postseason six straight years. Sugar could have joined returning senior and future NBA player, Sam Worthen. An All-American guard at Marquette, Worthen was known for his Rucker Tournament play.

Under their colorful coach Digger Phelps, Notre Dame had made the Final Four in 1978-1979. Returning seniors were Rich Branning and Bill Hanzlik, along with returning juniors Tracey Jackson, Kelly Tripucka, and Orlando Woolridge. If Sugar chose the Fighting Irish, he could join John Paxson, and fellow Michigander Tim Andree, as "diaper dandies" (i.e., talented freshmen). Plus, playing for the Fighting Irish would guarantee him a chance to play before a national television audience several times a year. Even if Notre Dame failed to qualify for the NCAA or NIT Tournaments.

Coach Ray Meyer's DePaul team had reached the Final Four in 1978-1979. Their squad consisted of returning two legendary Chicago players, sophomore Mark Acquire and junior Clyde Bradshaw. Joining Sugar would be fellow freshmen standouts, Terry Cummings, Teddy Grubbs, and Skip Dillard.

But not only Midwestern schools pursued him. After leaving the University of Detroit for San Diego State, David "Smokey" Gaines tried to coax Sugar to head west. Gaines had developed a relationship with Sugar when recruiting him at the University of Detroit. In addition to enjoying the nice weather, Sugar could have joined returning sophomore Tony Gwynn in the backcourt. Gwynn went on to have a hall of fame career in baseball with the San Diego Padres.

In Northern California, the University of San Francisco was mining for the treasure of Sugar's golden shooting touch. The swashbuckling Dons had made it to the second round of the NCAA tournament in 1978-1979. Their team included future NBA players Wallace Bryant, Bill Reid, and Guy Williams. Sugar would also be joining highly regarded freshmen Quintin Dailey, if he chose USF.

In the Lone Star State of Texas, Lamar University in Beaumont was hoping to lasso him to play for the Cardinals. With Coach Billy Tubbs, Lamar teams were known for their high scoring offense and full court press defense. Their 1978-1979 team had reached the second round of the NCAA tournament. With his offensive prowess and athleticism, Sugar would be a perfect fit for the Red Birds.

One intriguing school pursuing him was the University of Nevada in Las Vegas (UNLV). The Runnin' Rebels were renowned for an up-tempo style and stifling defense. Their long runs turned close games into blowouts under Coach Jerry Tarkanian's run-and-gun methods. After witnessing Sugar in a high school All-Star game, Tarkanian was like a ravenous shark chasing its prey. One of UNLV's incoming freshman was Sydney Green, New York City's 6'9" player of the year. Green would become an All-American and go on to a 10-year NBA career. In 1977, the Rebels had reached the Final Four in the NCAA Tournament. For Sugar, however, not only was UNLV a long way from home, but like Cincinnati, they were on probation for questionable practices. Sugar's dad advised him not to gamble on UNLV. Instead, he should hedge his bets, choosing a program with a cleaner reputation.

After careful consideration, Sugar was set to announce that he would sign with the University of Michigan. He had attended their camp the previous summer, along with other top players in the state, such as Mio's Jay Smith, who remains the all-time leading scorer in the history of Michigan high school basketball. Sugar was the Most Valuable Player of the camp. A couple of Michigan's top players, Phil Hubbard and Ricky Green, had given him a campus tour. He was quite impressed.

The weekend prior to his scheduled announcement, however, he received an anonymous phone call about a change in Michigan's staff. Jim Boyce, their top assistant coach, would leave to take over the head coaching job at Eastern Michigan University. The following Monday, Sugar expressed that he had heard that Coach Boyce was leaving Michigan for Eastern Michigan. Before deciding, he would wait and see whether this was true. Boyce assured him over the phone that he would be the assistant coach at Michigan throughout his college career.

Nevertheless, a few days later, Boyce departed Michigan's staff to become head coach of the Eastern Michigan Hurons (now Eagles). Sugar says in distaste, "He lied to me. He said he'd be there for my four years as an assistant coach. I had a chance to go all over the nation."[2] Boyce's decision didn't sit well with Sugar's former teammate at Creston, Bennette Gay, either. Bennette chose not to play for Boyce and Eastern his junior and senior years. The Wolverines immediately became extinct among Sugar's top choices of colleges.

In contrast, Central Michigan's assistant coach Dave Ginsberg had been a familiar presence to Sugar and his family. CMU's head coach Dick Parfitt had added Ginsberg as an assistant coach in 1975. As Ginsberg explains, "I sold the school every way I could. Every time Sugar turned around; I was standing there. I made him fall in love with the school."

Knowing Sugar's goal to play in the NBA, Gins boasted about former players. Ben Kelso, Jim McElroy, Ben Poquette, and Dan Roundfield went on to play in the NBA. In addition, two of Central's current stars, Leon Guydon and Val Bracey were products of Grand Rapids.

Parfitt had led the Chippewas to the NCAA Tournament in the 1974-75 and 1976-77 seasons. As a result, the team had generated a huge following, consistently playing to overflow crowds at home in Rose Arena. Plus, Central Michigan was close enough that Sugar's family could attend his home games, making Mount Pleasant even more pleasing.

But the ultimate seal on the deal to eventually sign with the Chippewas? Ginsberg's promise to always be there for him, even after his playing days were long over. He explains, "Loyalty was very important to a thoughtful and sensitive kid like Melvin." Sugar agrees. "The relationship with coach Ginsberg helped make my choice to come to Central Michigan."[3]

As the days got closer to his announcement date, scouts hounded Sugar, some calling him at five o'clock in the morning. Eventually, he stayed in other people's houses, just to get some rest. Just prior to his official signing, he was playing for the Michigan All-Stars in exhibition games in the Detroit area. Even there, four or five scouts were still shooting for a last-ditch win to get Sugar to play for their schools.

A press conference had been set up for him to make his announcement when he returned to Creston Auditorium in Grand Rapids. Sugar explained to the press after choosing Central,

 I liked coach Parfitt and coach (Dave) Ginsberg. I really respect them. Also, the people at Central were really warm and friendly each time I visited the campus. Also, I think it will be easy to adjust to college life on a campus like Central's. It is just a great situation there (at CMU). Val (Bracey) and Leon (Guydon, Battle Creek junior) also had a lot

to do with my choosing Central. Another factor is
that it is not too far away from my family to come
and see me play. They've been watching me play
my whole life and I wanted that to continue.[4]

Parfitt could hardly contain his joy after Sugar signed for
the Chippewas. "I don't think we've ever had this caliber of
player, a senior out of high school, at Central. James McElroy
was tremendously celebrated, and now he's with the New
Orleans Jazz. But Melvin is probably the best freshman we've
ever signed."[5]

With Melvin, incoming freshman included Don Wandzel, a
6'7" forward from Harper Woods, 6'3" Rob McQuaid from
Midland, 6'3" guard-forward Bill Cibulka of Dearborn, 6'5"
Gary Tropf from Holt, and Saginaw's 6'4" James Koger. Koger
had been captain of the Class A All-State team. Two junior
transfers would further bolster Central's lineup. Chicagoan
Mike Robinson, 6'9", came to Central via the University of
Michigan. Dan Mason brought his 6'6" frame from Joliet Junior
College in Illinois. Parfitt remarked, "We think it was a tremendous year for recruiting, but you can never tell how good it is
until they get here on campus."[6]

The caution behind Parfitt's optimism would prove
warranted during Sugar's four years at Central. Unfortunately,
they never quite lived up to their potential as a team, failing to
qualify for postseason play.

FIRING UP FOR THE CHIPS: "OH, MY!"

❝ An 'Oh My' is basically defined as a time where if you wandered away from the television set or the radio and you hear 'Oh My!' you ought to come running back in because it...is either a spectacular, unbelievable play that's either good or bad, a play that I've never seen before or a happening when you say how could someone do that at that crucial moment.

— DICK ENBERG, HALL OF FAME SPORTSCASTER
AND '57 CENTRAL MICHIGAN ALUMNUS

Four straight losing seasons created a dark era at Central Michigan. But in the darkness, Sugar was a bright light on the hardwood from 1979-1983.

Freshmen Season (1979-1980)

In his 1979-1980 season as a freshman, Sugar was second on the team in scoring. He followed 6'9" junior transfer Mike Robinson, averaging 12.4 points per game, while making 136 of 290 of his shots from the field at 49.9 percent. Most of his points came on his 25-foot jumper from the right side of the key. In addition, he contributed an average of two rebounds and 2.3 assists per game to add to his first-year resumé.[1]

The Chippewas lost their top three scorers and four of its five starters from their previous season's MAC co-championship squad. Surprisingly, they won eight of their first 11 games, including an opening season upset over the University of Detroit, 72 to 70. Eventually, though, the wheels came off. CMU finished the year with a losing record, going 6-10 in conference play, one game out of the playoffs, and 12-13 overall.

Sugar would wait patiently until his sophomore year to become Parfitt's go-to guy. In the meantime, when given the opportunity, he showed glimpses of his capability.

In a mid-January game at Bowling Green, he burst off the bench and got the hot hand from all over the floor. He would finish the game with a team-leading 24 points in a losing effort, 69 to 62. Later that month, in a game against Kent State, he made a buzzer-beating 10-foot, running, one-hand jump shot down the lane off an out-of-bounds play. That scored the Chippewas a sweet 73-71 Mid-American Conference victory on Parents' Day. Sugar's last-second dagger took place before a crowd of nearly 6,000 spectators at Rose Arena. This would be Sugar's first of a variety of game-ending winning shots while playing for the Chips. When talking after the game about his heroic shot, the smiling freshman felt great. "That was a good victory. I could feel it going in when I released it."[2]

In his final home game as a freshman, Sugar left Chippewa fans with a glimmer of hope for the next season. He went five-for-five from the field to help CMU get back in the game. They went on to defeat Bowling Green, 75-72. The Falcons' head coach John Weinert shook his head, muttering, "That number 14 (McLaughlin) made three shots while we were down by six.

If he would have missed there would have been a high bounce and we could have had some breakaways. It is a good thing this is not the NBA. Those would have been three-pointers."[3]

Sophomore Season (1980-1981)

Al McGuire, former Marquette Coach and basketball analyst, used to say of college basketball players that the best thing about a freshman is that they become a sophomore. They've already made the leap from high school to college their initial year. As a result, they're more equipped to face the challenges of being a student-athlete the following year.

Sugar emerged as the floor leader his sophomore year at Central in 1980-1981. He punished his opponents by making 231 of 460 shots (50.2 percent) for an average of 20.8 points per game (542 total).[4] His average was second in the conference behind Toledo's senior guard Harvey Knuckles' 20.9, who was selected the MVP. Central's main marksman scored 30 or more points in five contests. These featured a season high of 38 points against Bowling Green, 35 against Eastern Michigan, and 34 points against Ball State. As a result, league coaches selected Sugar for the Mid-American Conference First Team basketball squad.[5]

Of all the points scored in his collegiate career, his favorite memory took place that year. Two seconds remained in their last game of the season against the Ball State Cardinals. Central was down by one in overtime, 82-83. Sugar snatched the inbound pass from around the half court line. He spun by his rival defender, future coach Ray McCallum, dribbled once and launched a 40-foot shot before the buzzer sounded. Rose Arena erupted! The scoreboard advanced the home team's points to light up 84-83 in favor of the Chippewas. His buzzer beater deprived Ball State of the outright MAC title and gave Central Michigan a satisfying season-ending victory.[6]

Coach Ginsberg still marvels years later at how Melvin could possibly have gotten his shot off in time. He gives his first-hand account, as follows,

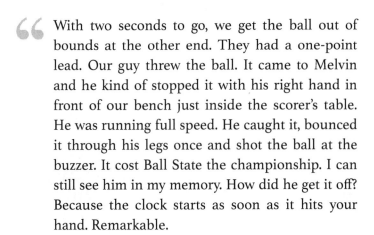

> With two seconds to go, we get the ball out of bounds at the other end. They had a one-point lead. Our guy threw the ball. It came to Melvin and he kind of stopped it with his right hand in front of our bench just inside the scorer's table. He was running full speed. He caught it, bounced it through his legs once and shot the ball at the buzzer. It cost Ball State the championship. I can still see him in my memory. How did he get it off? Because the clock starts as soon as it hits your hand. Remarkable.

"It was a beautiful, enthusiastic time," Sugar expresses.[7] To add to the beauty and enthusiasm of this highlight, he had 34 points and six rebounds for the night. A bittersweet victory, considering how Central's year ended, after the year's opening potential.

Central began the season impressively, defeating the University of Detroit and Michigan State to win the Cutlass Classic. Both victories were by 23-point margins. Sugar and 6'9" junior transfer Mike Robinson were named to the all-tournament team and Robinson was awarded the tournament's Most Valuable Player. Robinson combined with Sugar for 47 points in the championship game against the host Michigan State Spartans. Robinson had chipped in 26 points, while Sugar filled it up with 21 points. The Chippewas totally embarrassed the Spartans in their very first Cutlass Classic, 89-66. After the game Michigan State's Jud Heathcote was beside himself. "You talk about 'Downtown Freddie Brown' (former Seattle Super-sonic guard)—at Central they have 'Uptown Melvin McLaughlin.' He possesses great shooting range and is a threat anywhere in the front court. Definitely one of the great long-range shooters in the college game today."[8]

Sugar and Robinson gave Central a needed inside and outside game. Robinson played the role of Goliath, attacking the boards. Sugar played David, launching his sling-shot style jumpers from long-range. But when conference play began, things began to unravel. For the second year in a row, Central failed to make the seven-team cut for the conference tournament. They took ninth place in the MAC with a 5-11 league record.

They were close enough to win almost every game, losing in overtime to Toledo, Northern Illinois, and Ohio. The only exceptions were losses to Western Michigan in their season opener, 75-60, and to Northern Illinois in DeKalb, 70-57. James Koger's suspension at the midway point of the season, a lack of team cohesiveness, along with injuries to players Steve "Dr. Ram" Rambadt and Don Wandzel, only added to the team's misery.

Nonetheless, Sugar did his best to sweeten the bitter tears shed by the Chippewa faithful. At Bowling Green's Anderson Arena, he had a season-high 38 points, hitting 16 of 25 shots and adding seven free throws in a 96-95 loss. Ginsberg recalls,

 They had a box in one on Melvin. He had six points because he couldn't get his shot off. We're down by 20, playing against David Greer and Colin Irish. During a time out, Coach Parfitt says to Melvin, "Go to work and see what you can do." He scored 32 points in eleven minutes. It was so quiet in the arena, it was like somebody had just turned off the volume on a blaring radio. He was magic. If there had been a three-point play at the time, he would have had 60 points and we would have won by 10, because all of his shots were around the perimeter.

Against Miami of Ohio, Sugar hit 14-20 field goal attempts. He finished with a game-high 32 points, while handing off 12 assists. After the game, Miami Head Coach Darrel Hedric marveled, "McLaughlin is just fabulous. We don't have a ballplayer on our team that can stop him."[9]

Prior to the game against Eastern Michigan, Coach Jim Boyce was conciliatory. Indirectly responsible for Sugar becoming a Chippewa rather than a Wolverine, the coach said, "They (Central) probably have one of the best shooting guards in the country in McLaughlin." Sugar proved that in this case, Boyce could be trusted. He scored 35 points, while awing the Eastern Michigan fans with 30-footers at Bowen Field House in Ypsilanti. Afterward, Matt Dobek wrote in *Central Life,* "Is there a more exciting player in the conference than Melvin McLaughlin?"[10]

Against Kent State's man-to-man defense, Sugar showcased his offensive talents, scoring 32 points while passing for seven assists. On the other end of the court, his defense was like a lightning bolt against the Golden Flashes, resulting in four steals and five rebounds. Their head coach Ed Douma, in an attempt to stop him, changed strategies throughout the game, trying man-to-man, box-and-one, and zone defenses. But as he said with a sigh afterward, "We tried a lot of things. We couldn't stop him."[11]

Sugar became the fifth player in Chippewa history to score more than 500 points in one season. His 508 points matched James McElroy's total for fifth place in single-season scoring at CMU. At the time, McElroy was playing for the NBA's Atlanta Hawks.

Junior Season (1981-1982)

Central Michigan would be missing its seniors from the previous season. On top of that, three returning players announced they were transferring over the summer. One of these transfers was the much-heralded James Koger. This left the 1981-1982 squad even less experienced than they already were. The media picked the Chippewas to finish dead last in the Mid-American Conference. Their prediction would prove to be prophetic.

To make matters worse, Anthony Scott, Sugar's high school teammate at Creston, had been declared academically ineligible. Plus, Andy Kiss decided to transfer after the first semester, leaving the team with 10 players. The Chippewas ended up as the cellar dwellers in the MAC with a 4-and-12 record, and a 10-16 record for the season.

In spite of their losing record, Sugar inspired his teammates to strive for greatness regardless of the outcome. As he says, "Win or lose, you have to be great." The Chippewa cagers refused to quit in their role as conference spoilers. In an upset victory over Eastern Michigan in overtime, 68-66, Sugar pulled his teammates together. Rather than folding under the Hurons' attack, they charged right back down the floor with a dogged determination of their own.

In a re-match that the Hurons won 69-62, Eastern's Marlow McLain acknowledged, "Guarding Melvin McLaughlin man-to-man is tough because his range is 40-feet on in."[12] Coach Les Wothke's Broncos had defeated Central Michigan 82-67, holding Sugar to 24 points. After the game, Wothke admitted, "On an off day Sugar can still be the top scorer in the building."[13] For his third career last-second shot at Rose Arena, Sugar hit a 19-footer with one second to spare. As a result, Central Michigan upset Northern Illinois 64-62, a team picked to take second in the league.[14]

Though the Chippewas were far from being contenders, Rose Arena still buzzed with excitement because of its sweet-shooting star. He continued to fan the flames of the fired-up attitude of his fellow teammates. Though the key target of opposing defenses all year, Sugar's offensive prowess proved too much for his opponents. He led the conference in scoring, averaging 23.2 points per game while hitting 51.3 percent of his predominantly long-range shots. He broke the 30-point barrier seven times, and scored 44 points against Ball State. In addition, he finished the season with a career total of 1420 points, second in CMU and MAC history.[15] The six-foot guard led the 1981-82 Chippewas in five categories: field goals, free throws, points, assists, and steals. Deservedly, he was voted the Most Valuable Player in the MAC conference.[16]

Senior Season (1982-1983)

Going into his senior year, Sugar had piqued the curiosity of basketball fans nationwide. Most importantly, he drew the attention of NBA scouts. The 1982-1983 *Street and Smith Basketball Yearbook*, the "Bible" of college basketball, featured a picture of the 1982 MAC scoring leader and MVP. Sugar had arrived and expected to further elevate his status on the hardwood as a bona fide NBA prospect. As Coach Parfitt commented, prior to his senior year, "If Melvin continues to improve as he has his first three years, he should be a high draft pick."[17]

However, Parfitt also cautioned that his star guard had to improve defensively, adding, "He needs to be more physical." With that in mind, Sugar had worked out in the weight room during the summer months, confessing, "I definitely need to play better defense. I'm capable of it and have been working at it very hard. The coaches are really stressing 'D' (defense) this year. That and rebounding—our two biggest weaknesses last season."[18]

His senior season provided even more sweet memories of his playing days. Sugar went on to average 24.1 points, 3.2 rebounds, 3.1 assists, and 2.0 steals per game. He gave Chippewa loyalists reason to cheer, in spite of another losing season. Central finished 10-17 overall, 5-13 and ninth in the MAC.[19]

But what a show. McLaughlin tallied 21 points against Jim Boyce's Eastern Michigan Eagles, breaking CMU's all-time scoring record held by Ben Kelso. Afterward, Boyce lauded Sugar's stellar play in leading CMU's defeat against his Hurons. "Melvin showed what a great player he is. We played him tough on defense and he still got the ball to his teammates."[20]

During his final year, McLaughlin put together a 42-point performance in a 64-62 win over Toledo. On the road near the beginning stages of MAC play, he was 18-of-23 from the field and 6-of-6 from the free throw line. Following the game, Parfitt expressed, "It was vintage Melvin McLaughlin. That was as hot as I've seen him. He kept doing it even when he was fatigued."[21] Later in the season, McLaughlin canned a 23-foot jumper at the buzzer to beat Toledo, 70-69, at Rose Arena in Mount Pleasant. In a 74-68 home victory against Kent State, he tied his career high of 44 points. He was one point shy of the Rose Arena record set by Indiana State star Larry Bird in 1977.

But the game that stood out the most was his last home game at Central Michigan, when he eclipsed Bird's record. As Ginsberg recollects,

> The place was packed with people to see Melvin's last game. He was legendary on campus. The crowd during warm ups starting chanting, "Beat Bird! Beat Bird!" Such pressure. He goes out and scores 46 points. That son of a gun scored 46 points with no threes. That was breathtaking.

> There was ice water in his veins. The Ball State game was special, but that last home game when he beat Bird's record and set the arena record with all that pressure on him...phenomenal.

McLaughlin's stats for the night were 21 of 32 shots from the floor, four of six from the free throw line, five rebounds, two assists, and one steal. Bowling Green Coach John Weinert was asked if he had ever seen a shooter with better range or accuracy. He responded, "Well, I heard that God used to hit pretty good in a small gym in Jerusalem, but I never saw Him play, so I can't be sure. Melvin's probably No. 2."[22]

In spite of surpassing his stellar MVP season of the previous year, Sugar was unjustifiably left off the first All-Conference team. Just as at the BC camp, he was relegated to the second team. Coaches selected his nemesis at Ball State, Ray McCallum, as the league's 1983 MVP. Once more, Sugar appeared to be an obvious victim to the politics of basketball. He had outpointed and outplayed every opponent that year. He had led the league in scoring again, and was Player of the Week three times in the nine-week MAC conference season.

Years later, Ginsberg expresses his disbelief at the slight,

> Who knows why? Politics? The team's record probably. He didn't have a bad reputation. Some guys excel, but they're considered jerks, so some will hold that against them. But, Melvin's such a likable, humble guy. I don't know why anyone would have anything against him. Through the years, I've learned to focus on what you have control over. It was disappointing. But I told him, "This is not the first or the last disappointment you will have in your life." Life is a long journey and things pop up that cause you to shake your

head and ask, why? But ultimately, God's got a reason.

Equally confounding to Sugar's slight, is that there's hardly any film available of his seeing-is-believing performances. In my effort to find footage of Sugar's games at Central, I found an article in a 1983 *Central Life* student newspaper. It stated that CBS sports had been compiling a highlight film of his outstanding shots and moves. The film was to be shown during half-time of the NCAA championship game.[23] The two finalists that year were the sixth-seeded North Carolina State Wolfpack and the number one ranked Houston Cougars with stars Hakeem Olajuwon and Clyde Drexler. Jim Valvano's "Cinderella team" would upset Houston's "Phi Slama Jama" in one of the most memorable games in NCAA history.

Unfortunately, Sugar's half-time highlight film never materialized. If it did, over 32 million viewers would have gotten a taste of Sugar's unforgettably sweet moves on the hardwood.[24] Undoubtedly, this would have whetted their appetites for more Sugar!

In 1993, legendary Sports Broadcaster Dick Enberg and Sugar were inducted into Central Michigan University's Sports Hall of Fame. During his career, Enberg became well known for his signature on-air catchphrase, "Oh, my!" for particularly exciting and outstanding athletic plays. In his inception speech at the Banquet, Engberg expressed that the greatest regret of his Hall of Fame broadcasting career was never being given a chance to broadcast one of Sugar's games, and saying, "Oh, my!" over and over again on the airwaves throughout the contest.

18

EMBRACING THE CENTRAL SPIRIT

> To define "Central Spirit" is impossible. CMU students, however, know what it is, and all have it. Virtually anyone who meets or sees a CMU student or alumni, moreover, has a good sense of what it is. Central Spirit is pride in the university —the education received, campus, athletics, band, and everything that makes up CMU.
>
> — "CENTRAL SPIRIT," ESTABLISHED 1892

In December 1988, Charlie Coles, the head coach of Central Michigan's Men's Basketball Team, and his assistant coach Dave Ginsberg sit in a restaurant at their team's table in Las Vegas. They are there for the 1988 UNLV Miller Lite Rebel Round-Up, consisting of the men's basketball teams of Rhode Island, Central Michigan, Texas A & M, and the University of Nevada at Las Vegas.

Jerry Tarkanian is the host of the tournament and the legendary coach of the UNLV's Runnin' Rebels. Welcoming his visitors from the Great Lakes State, he ambles up to Central

Michigan's table. He recognizes Charlie Coles from recruiting one of his star players, Tony Smith, whom Coles had coached at Saginaw High School. Suddenly, his mind goes back to a sweet-shooting guard from Grand Rapids. For some reason or other, he ended up saying no to the allures of Sin City for the greener pastures of Mount Pleasant. He blurts out to Coles in his familiar raspy voice, "Central Michigan! That's where Melvin McLaughlin played!"

Coles, knowing Tarkanian had gone hard after Sugar in his recruiting efforts, starts to laugh and points his finger at assistant coach Ginsberg. "There's your problem. Right there! That's the one who got Melvin McLaughlin to go to Central Michigan!"

Tarkanian stares at Ginsberg. He's shocked at finally finding the guilty culprit responsible for snatching his highly coveted prospect from his clutches. He asks, "You're the one who recruited him?"

Ginsberg nods sheepishly. "Yep."

"Man, that kid could play." Tarkanian's face turns wistful. "He would have been treated like a god out here!"

While Sugar may not have been exactly deified, he was definitely revered on and off the basketball court in Mount Pleasant. Because he sees life through the lens of God's providence in his life, he has no regrets about his decision to play for Central Michigan. Instead, he's thankful to God for the experiences he had and the people he met there. The flame of the Central Spirit still burns as brightly within him as when he first stepped on campus as a freshman.

Along with his Hall of Fame career while playing for the Chippewas, he made lifelong friends at Central. He further solidified his bond with Dave Ginsberg, not only as a coach but as a faithful friend and mentor. In addition, he became "brothers from another mother" with teammates Sonny Newman, Derek Boldon and Kim Thompson. Plus, he knows that his mom would have been proud of his college career at Central Michigan University.

Nonetheless, there remains a question in the minds of many, "What if he had played for a different school rather than Central Michigan?"

Bob Becker was the sports editor for *The Grand Rapids Press* when Melvin played in high school and college. He's a member of the Michigan Sports Hall of Fame and the Grand Rapids Sports Hall of Fame, and is active with the American Legion. He showed up for our interview still dressed in his Legion uniform after assisting with a funeral. He is as bombastic in person, as I imagined him to be. And as opinionated as he was in print, I discovered that he's just as opinionated in person. He insists that Sugar's biggest mistake was choosing to play outside of the radar screen of a major media market.

 Central Michigan is wonderful and Dick Parfitt was a good coach, but no media came to Central Michigan games. If Mel had played for the University of Detroit, the *Detroit Free Press* and the *Detroit News* would have adopted him, because of his personality alone, plus they had nothing else going on at that point. Michigan and Michigan State weren't that good. They would have made a star out of Sugar. At Central, he got a great education, and did great there, but he got lost. There are bigger markets. In Detroit, he would have been an absolute star.

At Central Michigan, Sugar had to adjust to playing for a more traditional coach under Dick Parfitt. As the go-to guy in high school, Sugar was frustrated. Parfitt seemed to be squandering his talents, using him as a secondary player off the bench.

By his sophomore year, he earned a starting role. But even then, Parfitt's style of coaching didn't always mesh with Sugar's unique playing style. Parfitt stressed the importance of everyone touching the ball before taking a shot. Sugar says,

 You might pass the ball around for a minute and a half before somebody would even think about taking a shot. With a shot clock, we would have gotten plenty of shot clock violations. Every shot clock in the world would have buzzed off, with Parfitt shouting, "Everybody touch the ball!" Guys weren't even in the line-up and they had to touch the ball! Like, can we finally get a shot off?

Occasionally Parfitt had his team run a stall offense trying to eke out a win. This limited even more of Sugar's shots and scoring opportunities, much to his and his fans' consternation. With Parfitt, Sugar says, "Times had changed. Different types of ball (were) being played in the MAC. (Parfitt) played with his old philosophy too long. He had an old philosophy and had new-styled ball players."[1]

In fairness to Parfitt, Sugar was a twenty-first century style player, playing in the twentieth century. Some outliers included Tarkanian's Runnin' Rebels of UNLV (1973-1992) and Paul Westhead's highly potent Loyola Marymount teams (1985-1990). These were exceptions, though. For the most part, coaches followed the conventional style of a slower and more deliberate game of basketball. Fred Stabley became Central's Sports Information Director during Sugar's senior year. He assesses,

There may have been a little tension between Melvin's style of play and Parfitt's. Parfitt was old school and very successful, and I don't think he ever had a player like Melvin. He had four or five

NBA players, but most of them were big guys, and here comes Melvin who really had no conscience when it came to range. But I never saw any sign of disrespect from Melvin.

Even so, Parfitt was wise enough to make Sugar his go-to guy by his sophomore year with the Maroon and Gold. Ultimately, he wanted the ball in Sugar's hands for his last-second winning shots.

Making Mount Pleasant even less pleasant, was playing for a losing team for the first time in his life. Dave Ginsberg rues, "We just didn't have good chemistry during those years. We had great teams before him and great teams after him. We just missed the boat and I felt so bad for him, because he was a spectacular talent."

Yet, in spite of his discouragement, Sugar rose to the occasion as a wounded healer for his equally wounded teammates. A teammate and friend, Kim Thompson, saw his pain.

 Melvin was hurting, yet he was caring for us and encouraging us to all do better. I use my mom as an example. Even though she was sick, she would do things for other people who were sicker. None of us were equipped to deal with what we were going through. As I got older it dawned on me. Wow! What an incredible person he was and is.

Derek Boldon, former teammate and current friend, remembers Sugar's encouragement. In spite of the team's losing ways, Sugar never let them settle for less than their best. "He was like a coach on the floor in not letting his teammates get down on themselves."

Boldon and Sugar pushed each other to get better, sneaking into the football players' weight room to build strength. He still applies Sugar's motto "dare to be great" to his life endeavors. Boldon earned a second Master's degree in Health Science at USC in order to be an effective health administrator for Kaiser Permanente. During his twenty-year career coaching high school basketball in Southern California, Boldon often cited Sugar as an example to his players. He was always striving to get better. "Melvin is my brother from another mother, and his example for greatness remains with me all these years later."

Sugar also served as a mediator among his teammates. During his time at Central, the team had about the same number of black and white players. They had come from a variety of different backgrounds, ranging from inner-city Flint to rural Lima, Ohio.

Several key players either transferred or were suspended from the team. Even highly ranked recruit James Koger departed. This caused even more dissension among the ranks. In the midst of all this disarray, Sugar not only was the team's solid rock on the court. Off the court, he was like a faithful under-shepherd to his teammates. His compassionate and thoughtful leadership was as remarkable as his playing performances. Thompson says,

 We had eight black players and seven white players. There were clearly issues within the team. But Melvin could cross both lines. All these kids were making a big social adjustment. The black players had probably not been around too many white players and vice versa. Melvin saw that. He talked to and treated us all with equal respect. It didn't matter whether we were from a tough inner-city or a rural area. Melvin demonstrated to all of us, how to carry yourself. He was like a father to us. That's the kind of love and care he had for us.

Thompson also remembers Sugar's personal impact on his life as a student at Central, saying, "I'm not really a wild person. But you know how it can be in college when you're away from home on your own. One time he pulled me aside and talked to me about it. I saw the respect that he had for me and others when he spoke to us."

Sugar didn't merely hide out within the four walls of Rose arena; he stood out in the way he conducted himself all around Central Michigan's Mount Pleasant campus. Thompson further recalls,

> I learned a lot from him about character, when you think nobody sees you. People watched us off the court when we walked around campus. I saw Melvin interacting with people and signing autographs the way he does. None of those things showed up in the stats. Melvin had a very caring, generous personality and a pulse on what the other students were up to. What I learned from Melvin has helped me become a successful business man. I'm more conscious of others and my life's purpose. And that comes from being around Melvin McLaughlin.

Ron Sendre, Sugar's trainer at Central Michigan, says,

> Melvin was the kind of person that I would bring into my home any day that he needed. He could stay as long as he wants. You don't lose that personality. I have the highest respect for him. He was a genuine person and a genuine gentleman, even when he was in college. You can't say that about all the guys.

Dave Ginsberg lauds, "People on campus loved him and embraced him. His senior year, the students tossed those Sugar Packets when he was introduced before the games. They even created a PR poster and plastered it around campus and on their dorm room walls."

"He was special, beyond his basketball," Fred Stabley emphasizes. "He was humble, the kind of guy you rooted for. He competed and played hard, but he was a gentleman about it. I remember that smile. His smile went from ear to ear."

There are many "if only" and "what if" possibilities. What if Sugar hadn't attended CMU? He may not have heard about Scott McNeal's "Gus Macker 3 on 3 Tournament." McNeal, a 1979 CMU graduate, started the tournament along with some friends in his parents' driveway in Lowell, Michigan in 1974. But only after McNeal attended Central Michigan did the tournament begin to take off. He says, "We had a pipe line to Mount Pleasant during the tournament's heyday in the 1980s." Sugar was the Chippewa cager most responsible for putting the Gus Macker Tournament on the map. In Stabley's words, "Melvin was the King of the Gus Macker Tournament."

Sugar's statistics were amazing when firing it up for the Chips. Still, they pale compared to what they might have been with the three-point line. As Stabley articulates,

> With the three-point rule in, he might have led the nation. He could light it up like no other. The two others players I've seen who matched his range would be Jimmy Rayle from Indiana and Terry Furlow, who played in the NBA. I never saw anyone shoot it farther. Anytime he got past half court, Sugar was a threat.

Sendre echoes Stabley's sentiments, "If we had the three-point play then, he'd have surpassed any standing record by his junior year. Nobody could shoot like that guy, even today. You cross the ten-second line and you better be on him, because he's going to shoot it!"

"What a shame," Dave Ginsberg bemoans. "If the three-point play had been in effect, he would have been one of the top five scorers in the history of college basketball. Probably 40% of his baskets were threes. That's a lot of points!"

Bobbie stresses,

 Until this day his record has not been broken at Central Michigan University and that was before the three-point shot. What if they had the three-point shot when he scored over 2,000 career points? That's a phenomenal number that would still be intact today. I'm talking nationally not just at his university. So, add those extra points per game to his number. Are you talking another 1,000 points?

Adding to his big brother's claim, Sugar says, "Here's another thing. I never played in any post-season tournament games like a lot of the players do. I did this all in regular season games."

Ultimately, Kim Thompson points to the source of his former teammate's talent. "There was a special grace about him when he played. You could tell that he wasn't doing what he did on his own. God was with him. I've never seen anybody play the way he played with such joy and peace. He was in a whole different element than everyone else on the playing floor."

What if he'd played for a higher profile school and/or for a program that had qualified for the post-season NCAA tournament? Sugar might have been given a greater chance of fulfilling his dream of playing in the NBA. Nonetheless, Sugar remains proud of his time at Central Michigan and his now-retired Number 14. His Sugar Mel Basketball Camp bears the Chippewa maroon and gold. His legacy lives on in those who saw him play and the lives he touched while at Central.

When his mom named him "chief" (aka Melvin), little did she know that her son would become the chief of the Chippewas' basketball team. And to the lingering question, "What if he had gone to a different program?" Sugar and his brother Bobbie both answer, "God has a plan." God had a reason for allowing Sugar to play for the Chippewas. Even now He's still working things out for good according to His purposes. Sugar's role is to follow the plan of his life's Head Coach, confident that a setback is His setup for a comeback.

Sugar embodies the Central Michigan Spirit in his loyalty to the maroon and gold. The University's official seal contains CMU's motto in Latin, *Sapientia, Virtus, Amicita:* Wisdom, Virtue, and Friendship. In the midst of playing under adverse conditions at Central Michigan, Sugar displayed all three virtues. He continues to pass them down to the kids at his basketball camps and in the community.

Central Michigan University has produced its share of NBA players. But none have quite the same aura of a sweet-shooting guard wearing Number 14. He embodied the Central Spirit both on and off the court.

19

SUGAR'S DREAM TURNS SOUR

66 Melvin could have played in the NBA. There's no question about it. One scout told me that really only 30% of the players are the elite ones. The other 70% could be replaced by others just as good as they are. It's just a matter of being in the right location. You may be good enough, but it's somebody else's decision whether or not you wear that team's uniform, not yours.

— DEREK BOLDON, SUGAR'S TEAMMATE AT
CENTRAL MICHIGAN

Since 1998, in agreement with the National Basketball Players Association, the NBA draft has been limited to two rounds. Undrafted players may try out for any team. In lieu of using their draft picks for players, teams can also opt to trade draft picks for players, for money, or for other draft picks. In the league's early years, teams simply selected players until they ran out of prospects. Eventually, the draft was organized into specific rounds.

But when the 1983 NBA draft took place, 226 players were selected over ten rounds by the league's 23 teams. The Cleveland Cavaliers selected Sugar in the sixth round, the 119th player in the draft. It had been speculated that Sugar would be picked between the third and fifth rounds. Why the late selection? Likely Central Michigan's subpar performances during his four-year career and failure to qualify for post-season play.

Cleveland Cavaliers

Cleveland had already selected nine players in the earlier rounds of the draft. Even so, Sugar felt confident that, given the opportunity, he would be able to fulfill his lifelong dream of playing in the NBA. He told *The Grand Rapids Press*, "There's definitely no doubt about my abilities. I'm gonna go down there with a confident attitude and treat it as a serious business. We're all ballplayers and just because someone went to a bigger school doesn't make them a better ball player."[1] The Cavaliers never gave him a chance.

The Cavs first round picks were Roy Hinson (Rutgers) and Steward Granger (Villanova). Second round picks John Garris (Boston College) and Paul Thompson (Tulane) monopolized the court throughout their camp. In addition, Cleveland's returning veteran players left him little room to crack the lineup.

Further, one of their veteran players, who struggled with a drug addiction at the time, was also being considered. He took a brief furlough from the league to recover. Afterward, his former Houston coach, Tom Nissalke, offered him another chance to revive his career at Cleveland. Eventually he would triumph over his addiction. He became a leading advocate in helping other NBA players overcome similar addictions.

But when Sugar was trying out for the Cavs, it was evident to everyone that this player still struggled with drugs. The veteran player pulled Sugar aside and confessed, "You know I go to drug addiction meetings. But I'm thinking about doing a line all the time. I know I can't, because they're watching me."

Sugar was in tip-top condition. He thought, "Why is this cat even here? Why isn't he in a drug rehab center getting help like he's supposed to get?" It didn't seem fair, that this drug addict be considered for the team. Meanwhile, Sugar was overlooked, though treating his body like the temple of the Holy Spirit.

To add to this injustice, over lunch Coach Nissalke disclosed to Sugar that this player was in the camp to help his son, Tommy Jr., learn to play tennis. In addition to being an All-American in basketball, the struggling player had also been an All-American tennis player in college. Sugar recalls thinking, "He's taking someone's spot, all because he can teach the coach's son how to play tennis, and he's got a contract? He's not in good health even though he's supposed to be getting well." Now, he says,

> "They got me out there and I never really played in a game. It was always a little bit of time here and a little bit of time there, so I didn't get a fair shot. It felt like a waste of my time even being there. I asked myself, 'Why am I here? Take me home!'"

It appears the Cleveland basketball organization was in an equal state of disarray. That season the Cavs would go 28-54, firing Nissalke mid-season the following year. Whether or not his son, Thomas Nissalke, Jr., went on to become a tennis star as result of the tennis lessons is unknown.

184 | REV. DR. VERNON E. WENDT, JR.

Detroit Pistons

His boyhood home team picked up Sugar as a free agent. Finally, an opportunity to prove he belonged among basketball's elite players! During the Detroit Pistons camp, he wowed players and media alike with his shooting skills and overall game. Since he was originally from nearby Ann Arbor, the TV and newspaper reporters gravitated to him. They crowded around after practices for interviews and pieces in their columns.

His infectious play garnered much media attention. Sugar says, "I'm killing it in the camp and had a really good practice. Afterward, I got so many interviews. Because I'm from Ann Arbor, when I got to camp, I was the focus of all these cameras."

Vinnie Johnson kept saying to him, "Rook, they're treating you like a veteran. We can't get interviewed, because you're getting all the interviews!" Some players started to rag on Isiah Thomas, saying, "Sug lit a torch up your butt today!" "He's going to take your spot!" "Sugar's going to be the franchise player, not you!" Isiah could only laugh off the insults, saying, "Yeah, I know, Sugar's going to be the franchise player this year, not me." By this time, Sugar says, everyone was bursting out laughing at Isiah's expense.

Like Sugar, Thomas had graduated from high school in 1979, but already had two years in the league after leading the Indiana Hoosiers to a national championship in 1981. Thomas wasn't the shooter that Sugar was, but was one of the most competitive and fearless players in the NBA. Called "The Baby Assassin," Isiah's youthful look and cherubic smile belied the fact that in spite of his 6'1" stature, he would back down to nobody. Thomas would lead the Pistons to NBA World Championships in 1989 and 1990. They were nicknamed "The Bad Boys" for their aggressive and intimidating basketball style.

Coach Richard Daly was nicknamed "Daddy Rich" for his

coiffed hair style and expensive designer suits that he wore while coaching on the sidelines. Daly had just been hired by General Manager Jack McCloskey in May, hoping "Daddy Rich" could reverse the trend of the Pistons' previous six losing seasons. Ultimately, Daly was seen as the one to lead the Pistons out of their bondage of futility and into the promised land. He would help them win an NBA championship and hoist the coveted Larry O'Brien trophy above their heads. He demanded and cajoled his team to become a unit of hardwood gladiators, allowing no easy baskets in their quest for victory. In contrast, Sugar was labeled a weak defender, though he had consistently led his team in steals at Central Michigan. Besides, he had the foot speed to match just about any player in the NBA.

After his showing at the Pistons' camp, Sugar realized, "I can play with these guys just like I did in high school and college. They're no different." However, similar to Sugar's experience at the BC camp while in high school, the Pistons had predetermined the results of his team tryout. In essence, they considered him a practice player. He was to help the returning veterans, new players with guaranteed contracts, and highly regarded rookies get ready for the season.

In hindsight, signs all along revealed Sugar's lame duck candidacy for wearing the Pistons' royal blue, red, and white uniform. In fact, Coach Daily whispered in his ear when he first arrived to practice, throwing down the gauntlet. "To make this team, you're going to have to beat out Isiah." Sugar thought, "Right, Chuck. You're asking me to beat out the franchise player of this team who already has a guaranteed contract?"

Isiah's position as the returning Pistons' starting point guard was a foregone conclusion. However, Sugar had already proven he could beat one of their guards in head-to-head competition in MAC conference play, "Walker D." Russell, a former Western Michigan standout. Sugar was light years ahead as a player, but Walker D. had played one year already with the Pistons. Some veteran players made him their lackey as a rookie, and indicated to McCloskey they wanted to keep him around.

Also, Russell had been a local star in high school at nearby Pontiac Central. His oldest brother, Frank, had played at the University of Detroit and later with the Chicago Bulls for a season. His other brother, Campy, had been an All-American at Michigan and went on to star for the Cavaliers, until injuries shortened his career. Hence, Walker D. had the additional advantage of wearing the Russell name on the back of his jersey, which helped sell tickets.

As Sugar learned the hard way, the goal of an NBA team isn't necessarily winning, it's putting fans in the seats. Players are often chosen not only because of their talent. They're also on the team because of their owner's sense of their appeal to fans, media, and advertisers.

A glaring example of Walker D.'s favored status with the Pistons' organization took place after Sugar sank several long-range shots over him in a scrimmage. McCloskey had been watching their duel from the stands. During the water break, he furiously marched down to the court and ran up to the outmatched Russell. Getting into his face, he screamed, "You're going to let that little pipsqueak score on you all day like that? That little runt hit five jump shots in a row on you right in your face. You did nothing to stop him. Do something different to him! If you got to poke him in his eye, do it, but you got to do something different!"

Walker D. was so embarrassed, he didn't talk to Sugar the rest of the camp. The players stifled their laughter at Walker's chastisement by the team's owner. Sugar thought, "Why is Walker D. being scolded and I'm being totally ignored?" He reflects now, "I knew no matter how I did in camp; I was in jeopardy. Rather than wanting the best player, the owner was against me, which I'm still trying to figure out."

Consequently, he wasn't surprised to be cut from the team. This time, however, he could hold his head high. He had proved he belonged in the NBA while going against some of the top players in the league. News reporters asked McCloskey why Sugar was released from the team in spite of his outstanding play in the tryouts. McCloskey admitted that he was "an unbelievable scoring machine." But then he added, the growing trend of the league was to have 6'8"-6'9" guards like Magic Johnson.

Vinnie Johnson earned the nickname "The Microwave" for his ability to heat up quickly, when coming off the bench. Immediately after Sugar's release from the team, The Microwave sought him out and said in front of everybody.

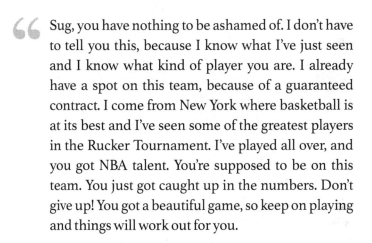

Sug, you have nothing to be ashamed of. I don't have to tell you this, because I know what I've just seen and I know what kind of player you are. I already have a spot on this team, because of a guaranteed contract. I come from New York where basketball is at its best and I've seen some of the greatest players in the Rucker Tournament. I've played all over, and you got NBA talent. You're supposed to be on this team. You just got caught up in the numbers. Don't give up! You got a beautiful game, so keep on playing and things will work out for you.

Consoled by Vinnie's thoughtfulness, Sugar says, "I respect Vinnie Johnson to this day, because he was so real and genuine. He knew what he had just seen. And coming from him as a pro, I felt validated."

Leaving the Pistons' camp, Sugar thought with satisfaction,

"I've proven to others that I belong in the league. It just wasn't meant to be." Although God's unexpected detour didn't stop him from pursuing his dream of playing in the league; there were other routes. Perhaps Sugar reasoned at the time, "I might just launch my NBA career by being a star in the CBA?"

The Continental Basketball Association was the Official Development League of the NBA for most of the 1980s and 1990s. The league was a training ground of future NBA coaches and players. (Consider Phil Jackson, George Karl, Michael Adams, John Starks and Tim Legler). It also became the last resort for players whose careers had faded due to drugs, injury, or unmet expectations (e.g., Lloyd Daniels, John Drew, Michael Ray Richardson, Roy Tarpley, and Chris Washburn).[2]

Detroit Spirits

The CBA Detroit Spirits immediately acquired the rights to Sugar from the Lancaster Lightning (PA) and signed him in October of 1983. The Spirits, led by General Manager Sam Washington, who ran the city's legendary St. Cecilia's summer basketball league, had been one of the first minority-owned sports franchises. They filled a void in the city, left when the Pistons moved their games to the Pontiac Silverdome. In their inaugural season of 1982-1983, the Spirits won the CBA championship.

Initially, it appeared to be a win-win situation for both Sugar and the defending champs. Coach Gary Mazza boasted, "His range is really good. I already knew he could shoot anywhere inside of Eight Mile."[3] In a press release, Washington said he was pleased to have Melvin on his team. He crowed, "This is the only guy that I won't challenge in H-O-R-S-E. His range really is that good."[4] He predicted Sugar to be the main reason for the Spirits to repeat as the CBA champions. Most importantly, Washington projected, "He is going to set the league on fire. 'Sugar' is totally unselfish when it comes to who has the basketball. 'Sugar' will be in the NBA this year or next year."[5]

From the beginning, however, the former CMU sensation sensed something wasn't right. During an initial intra-squad scrimmage, Sugar demonstrated his outside shooting prowess over and over. Rather than becoming excited about joining forces in an arsenal attack of outside shooters, Kevin Smith and Tico Brown whined to Coach Mazza. Brown, not Sugar, was to be the main source of the Spirit's outside scoring. Furthermore, Smith's assists and playmaking skills were to compliment Brown, not Sugar.

According to Sugar, Mazza was insecure about keeping his job. Rather than relying on him as the go-to person on the team, he chose to go with the returning star players. In spite of Mazza's and Washington's accolades, Sugar was cut after only three games. During those three games he hardly broke a sweat on the playing floor. Sugar says,

Mazza called after our second loss to Wisconsin, saying his job was in jeopardy. He wanted to go with experience rather than youth. I had been promised just as much playing time as starting guards Smith and Brown, but I wasn't getting it. I was released for the coach's personal sake.

Even more disappointing, behind the scenes Sugar discovered that many of the Spirits battled drug addictions. Once, on the team bus to a game against the Wisconsin Flyers in Oshkosh, coaches drove in a separate car. On the way to the game, some players started smoking weed and getting high. "It was unbelievable and hypocritical," Sugar says. "How can they even play? I can't explain how I felt, I was so miffed. I broke out with a rash, there was so much smoke on the bus. The players and coaches did nothing. They let them do what they wanted. I was on the phone that night, saying, 'Get me out of here!'"

One teammate showed Sugar the heroin track marks up and down his arms. Once selected in the fourth round of the NBA draft by a top franchise in the NBA, he was let go for doing heroine in their camp. After playing overseas, he had made a relatively successful comeback playing for the Spirits the previous year. Sugar had wondered privately, "How can he play?" His brief stint with the Spirits answered the question. The player was only half with-it in their games. In spite of his talent and size, he was cut from the team along with Sugar.

Mazza was fired the following spring, after the Spirits' elimination from the play-offs. The team eventually floated off to Savannah, Georgia after the 1985-1986 season.

On the Rebound

In spite of three successive failures in trying out for teams, Sugar remained determined. "I certainly had my share of disappointments in the last half-year. But it's those who can overcome adversity that come out ahead. And I intend to do just that."[6] Sugar found some consolation by working on his bachelor's degree in Community Recreation. "You can't play basketball forever. A degree is something I can earn which can't be taken away from me due to someone else's insecurity."[7] After that, he explains, "I came home, and chilled away from basketball for a while, because of the political mess I got involved in. When you're better than anyone, you're supposed to be picked over them. I got unhappy with the game of basketball for a minute there."

But only for a brief minute, at that. Bobbie called, encouraging him to come out and play in the 1984 summer pro league in California. Once again, Sugar shined on the playing floor, earning the league's Most Valuable Player. He drew the attention of several agents who advised him of his options, including playing overseas. A team in the Philippines offered a $100,000 contract, the equivalent of nearly $260,000 in 2020. Plus, he might have capitalized on his popularity, by making even more money from endorsements. However, the country was on the verge of a revolution and civil unrest due to the impending overthrow of President Ferdinand Marcos. "The Pearl of the Orient" didn't appear to be a safe place to live.

Similar offers arose from teams in other countries. But "wars and rumors of war" made Sugar reluctant to become "a stranger in a strange land," even with his familiar friend of basketball to accompany him. At the time, the Cold War showed no signs of getting any warmer. The United States had boycotted the 1980 Summer Olympics held in Moscow in protest of the 1979 invasion of Afghanistan. In turn, the Soviet Union and its allies would boycott the 1984 Summer Olympics in Los Angeles.

The spread of communism threatened our national security. President Reagan attempted to stop it by providing financial and military aid to anticommunist governments and insurgencies around the world. It made for tense times. Both Russia and the United States feared being attacked by each other and were preparing to interrupt these attacks. Playing overseas didn't appear worth the risk to Sugar. He quips, "I wanted to wear a basketball uniform, not a military uniform."

On top of that, the common route at the time was to go directly from college stardom to the NBA, rather than a detour overseas. Few foreigners had made the NBA in the 1980s. Most who reached the league, like Detlef Schrempf (Washington) and Hakeem Olajuwon (Houston), had played college ball in the USA. Sugar's nephew Quinn shares, "When my uncle didn't make the NBA, he wasn't motivated to play overseas, though he would have made a lot of money. For him it was either the NBA or bust."

One agent wanted him to play with the San Diego Clippers, where he'd work out with recently traded Los Angeles Laker All-Star, Norm Nixon. Another agent fell in love with him after seeing him make a move that literally left him speechless. He promised him a tryout with the Houston Rockets. However, being a practice player for the pre-determined teammates didn't interest Sugar. He knew he'd be released after they finished using him for their purposes. No matter how brightly they shine, as a free agent in the NBA, a diamond in the rough has little chance to be discovered. Particularly when competing against players already slotted for a team's roster.

Besides that, he was a family man through and through. Back in Grand Rapids, Linda waited for him, along with his family. He realized that as the head of the household, he was to provide for his future family. His dad had responded to the deaths of his wife and older daughter by shouldering the burden of becoming a godly father. Similarly, Sugar responded to the death of his NBA dream by becoming a godly father like his dad. His son, Melvin Jr. (aka "Pooh" and "Little Sugar") was born in 1988, and his beautiful daughter, Morgan, in 1996. Their beaming faces were visible reminders to return home. Even though he was disappointed, he found hope in Jesus' promise, "Come to me, all you who are weary and burdened, and I will give you rest. Take my yoke upon you and learn from me, for I am gentle and humble in heart, and you will find rest for your souls. For my yoke is easy and my burden is light" (Matthew 11:28-30).

Sugar recognized deep in his heart that God had a greater purpose for giving him his love and talent for basketball than fortune and fame. Abraham had faith to offer up his beloved son Isaac to God, confident that He would resurrect him if he did. Resolute, Sugar had faith to offer up his dream of NBA stardom to God. God would resurrect it into something sweeter than he had even thought of or imagined.

20

A BALLER FOR LIFE

> Basketball isn't just about the bright lights, packed arenas and highlight reels. Basketball is a way of life. Basketball is a relationship between you and the ball, you and your teammates. If you love the game, nobody can take that from you.
>
> — MICHAEL JORDAN

Returning to Grand Rapids, Sugar was severely disappointed that he wasn't given a fair chance in his professional tryouts. He could have soured on the game of basketball altogether, regretting his investment in this sport. He could have told himself he was a failure, or that he should have focused on another sport. Sugar was and is a remarkably gifted athlete, and excelled in most every sport he played. As he jokes, with a tinge of sadness, "I could have been in the Olympics!"

But switching sports was not an option. Basketball was not only his love, it was part of his DNA. He knew, above all, that God had given him this insatiable love for the game as well as his phenomenal ability to play the game. God could use both, for His purposes. Even with his NBA dream shattered, Sugar trusted God. He could put the pieces of his basketball life together into a beautiful picture of His grace. Besides, just as some of the players in his tryouts were addicted to drugs, Sugar had his own addiction problem. He couldn't possibly quit playing basketball. The God Thing that had been instilled in him at age four continued to be at work in him. He has given Sugar both the power and desire to play the game for His good pleasure (see Philippians 2:13). Through basketball, Sugar was able to inspire and influence others in the community.

He turned to Linda for comfort. With her, he opened up about the difficulty of growing up without his mom. He remembered how he used to reconnect with his mother after her death. He'd head to the basketball court, where he would experience a foretaste of his heavenly home. Playing on the courts rekindled Sugar's relationship with his mom. The epiphany-like moments of the game centered him. He knew again the sense of God's glory, launching those long-range jumpers. A glory punctuated by the swooshing sound of basketballs rippling the nets.

His NBA dream soured, but his love for basketball only sweetened. No longer was he under the constraints of being evaluated by those who didn't appreciate his style of play. Sugar found renewed peace and joy playing for God and for His glory.

While his dad found solace in his hunting trips, Sugar would find solace in hunting for open courts and fellow hoopsters to play with. Just as his dad, who passed away in 1989, was noted for his marksmanship in shooting for wild game, so his youngest child continues to be noted for his shooting marksmanship while playing the game of basketball. However, unlike his dad, who was the main cooker in the family, Sugar isn't interested in spending a lot of time in the kitchen. He'd prefer to spend his time playing basketball. Instead, God has blessed him with Linda, who provides him with plenty of delicious meals to keep him well-nourished. Although, you'd never guess it by his trim physique.

This diamond continued to shine, playing semi-professionally and in various exhibition games such as the annual TA-WA-SI game. In the 1990 Summer NBA Pro-Am League, Sugar played for the Debut team, featuring former NBA player Dennis Bell, Marquette's Michael "Pops" Simms, CMU's Vern Anderson, Grand Valley State's Greg Pruitt, and Jay DeVries. He averaged 46 points in the league.[1] While leading Debut to the Michigan Recreational State Championship title, he scored a record-breaking 50 points in the championship game. In three games he netted 150 points, setting another record. His exploits earned him the Most Valuable Player award.[2] And at the age of 30, he customarily scored over sixty points in the Flint summer pro league.[3]

The Gus Macker 3 on 3 Tournament

Sugar's "wowing" days were far from over, though many occurred closer to his hometown courts. On March 31, 1974, a group of teenagers in Lowell, Michigan, came up with an idea to have a three-on-three basketball tournament to coincide with the NCAA Finals weekend. They named this the Gus Macker Tournament, after a nickname given Scott McNeal by a junior high friend, Rick Thompson. McNeal reveals how Thompson came up with his famous moniker, as follows:

 My last name is McNeal, so I've been called Mack a lot. At the time Gus Ginakas coached at Michigan State. Rick combined Gus with the last name Mack, and came up with Gus Macker. It didn't have a lot of significance. Although some people are a little let down when they discover

that the 6'8" black guy they imagined being Gus
Macker is really a 5'8" white guy.

The original Gus Macker Tournament involved six teams
making a total of 18 teenage "Lowellians." Each player dropped
a dollar in the pot. Using the McNeal driveway as the tournament basketball court, they battled it out, three-on-three style.
The winning team split the eighteen dollars. In its second year,
the tournament grew from 18 to 30 players, and 36 in its third
year. "Then the athletic director called to tell us that someone
could lose their amateur status," McNeal remembers. "We
decided to play for trophies, and expand the event from my
mom's driveway into the streets."

For the next several years, the annual Gus Macker Tournament consisted of local players. However, through connections
McNeal made while attending Central Michigan University,
graduating in 1979, the tournament began to expand. To
McNeal's surprise and delight, one of McNeal's classmates at
Central, who had also been his classmate at Lowell, brought
the Grand Rapids' product and Central Michigan star Leon
Guydon to play in the tournament. McNeal says, "That's when
we decided to put really good players in separate brackets from
the rest of the players in the tournament."

For the following year's tournament, Guydon brought a
Central Michigan teammate, Val Bracey, and his brother Tim.
Tim played for Eastern Michigan at the time. Their fourth
player was Tom Crean, an unlikely eighth grader from Mount
Pleasant. Crean didn't see any playing action on the court, but
was a key contributor to the team's success in the tournament.
He found their first financial backer, getting his mom to pay
their entry fee. He also successfully begged her to drive the
players back and forth from Grand Rapids to the tournament. Crean spent that weekend camping out in the McNeal
family room. He went on to coach at the Division I level for

Indiana University, and took Marquette to the final four with Dwayne Wade. Currently, he is head coach for the University of Georgia. That 1979 Gus Macker Tournament might be considered Crean's unofficial coaching debut.

But the Chippewa to have the most impact on the tournament's growth and success was Sugar McLaughlin. He learned of the tournament his sophomore year. He says, "Val Bracey and Leon Guydon told me that I need to play in the Macker tournament. I didn't think we could play, because of the NCAA rules, but I played anyway." During college in 1981, Sugar first entered the tournament. Sure as his shooting, crowds gathered to watch his sweet moves and unparalleled shooting skills. Even when the wind picked up, Sugar's shot found its mark, again and again.

Parfitt's reaction was predictable. Sugar says, "When Coach Parfitt got wind of it, he got so mad. He thought I would be ineligible. He sure scolded me at his office. 'You could cost yourself a season and some tournament games!' But Gus (McNeal) reassured him that the tournament was NCAA-sanctioned."

Word spread. Other area-wide college and local high school players soon entered the tournament. In its early years, the Gus Macker Tournament was like the Grand Rapids version of the famed New York City's Rucker Tournaments. Area legends gathered to play at the Macker. On top of that, people could witness Sugar do his thing up close and in person. McNeal still marvels over 45 years after his tournament's start. "All this was going on in my parents' driveway!"

Thanks to a loyal fan base in Grand Rapids, the Gus Macker Tournament eventually became so big that to oversee its expansion in the late '80s, McNeal had to quit his job as a teacher and basketball coach. An article on Laguna Beach basketball tournaments, and other outdoor venues, appeared in *Sports Illustrated (SI)*. Those events featured only 20 to 30 teams. After seeing the article, one of McNeal's neighbors, Jeff Stormzand, in eighth or ninth grade at the time, stormed, "What about us?" The Gus Macker at the time had hundreds of teams in their tournament. Compelled to send a handwritten letter to the magazine, Stormzand emphasized *SI*'s blatant omission.

McNeal says, "We told him nobody from *Sports Illustrated* was going to read his handwritten letter. But it was picked up by a guy named Alexander Wolff!"

Surprisingly, Wolff calmed any further storms resulting from the magazine's oversight with a visit in the summer of 1984, exploring a possible story on the Gus Macker 3 on 3 Tournament in Lowell. The trip's impetus, in addition to Stormzand's letter, included Wolff's cross-country research for his book on playground basketball courts and players throughout the nation, *The In-Your-Face Basketball Book*. Wolff absolutely fell in love with the tournament. In tiny Lowell, Michigan, all kinds of people of different ages, backgrounds, races, and genders, united together as one. Their common goal? To play or watch the basketball games. To paraphrase Galatians 3:28, there was neither black or white, yellow or red, short or tall, old or young, guard or forward or center, baller or hacker. All were one at the Macker Tournament in a mutual love for basketball.

Editors at *SI* cut Wolff's original and enthusiastic 12-page article down to two or three pages. Wolff lobbied for nearly a year to convince his editors to publish a lengthier article, finally published in July of 1985. Wolff highlighted Sugar and his gunslinger style of play, including his game-winning "Hindenburg shot" in 1982. McNeal says, of that famous shot,

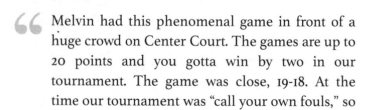

Melvin had this phenomenal game in front of a huge crowd on Center Court. The games are up to 20 points and you gotta win by two in our tournament. The game was close, 19-18. At the time our tournament was "call your own fouls," so

there was a lot of arguing over calls and hacking throughout the game. Then Melvin hit this shot from as far back as you can be on the driveway while falling back into the crowd. The crowd had so many oohs and ahhs, it sounded like we had just witnessed a brilliant firework display on the Fourth of July.

Wolff's article generated a huge response. The Gus Macker Tournament elevated from being a local tournament to a nationally known event. According to McNeal, "That summer the tournament had people from all over the country as we became part of Wolff's quest to find unique places to play pickup games of basketball." In addition, McNeal remarks, "ABC's *World News Tonight* did a feature on the Macker. In the clip, the *World News Tonight* guy is talking, and then they do a quick interview with Sugar. Afterward they show about twenty seconds of him playing to the background of the Harlem Globetrotter song, 'Sweet Georgia Brown'."

In the mid-80s there were 88 courts strung up and down with wooden little hoops, featuring divisions of all levels of play. Players and their teams were ranked from little kids to retirees to college and professional players. But the main draw of the Macker tournament was Sugar and his shooting prowess. It was as if his basketball had a magnetic pull to the center of the basket. Crowds were consistently dazzled at his ability to get his shot off against all kinds of defensive sets, in spite of the summer heat and wind currents.

Eventually, the tournament outgrew tiny Lowell in drawing over 4,000 players and spectators, forcing a move to nearby Belding. Despite the tournament's departure from The Showboat City, Sugar continued to showboat his basketball skills, delighting Macker crowds for years. In fact, he was so popular that its first year in Belding, his team was forced to forfeit due to being stuck in traffic. In all likelihood, that very traffic jam was due to the masses of people driving to Belding at the same time in order to see him play!

His crowd-pleasing play continued to wow—and to win. In one game, Sugar scored nineteen of his team's twenty points against a team from Illinois, leaving them utterly stunned. They had never heard of him before! In another highlight, he nearly replicated his legendary Hindenburg fall-away. While landing into the surrounding crowd, he made another game-winning shot.

From the original six teams, the tournament peaked with 5378 teams in 1992. Due to complaints regarding the excessive physical play by some of the players, it eventually waned a bit. McNeal and his staff chose to reinvent the tournament to be more family oriented, and not worry about having a monstrous number of teams. More adults began to bring their kids to play in what might be described as a kinder, gentler version of the Macker Tournament.

Today, the Macker is more user-friendly, with hired officials to keep rough play and complaining at bay. Although there have been changes, the goal of the tournament remains the same. Have fun playing basketball as a gift from God to enjoy. In spite of being cut from his junior high basketball team, McNeal continues to love the game. He's found a kindred spirit in Sugar, who continues to love basketball in spite of being cut from the NBA.

In the Gus Macker Museum on Main Street in Belding, MI, McNeal dedicated a whole wall to Sugar, along with an entire room filled with various pictures and displays of Sugar in action. After all, "The King of the Gus Macker Tournament" helped put McNeal's Gus Macker Tournament on the map!

McNeal, now in his 47th year of the tournament, plans to hit 50 years before he talks about an exit strategy. Although he adds, "It will still happen, whether I'm rolling out there in a walker or not." After all, McNeal quips, "They say if you can't play the game, coach, and if you can't coach, start your own tournament." Sugar, the shooting star who helped launch the tournament into orbit, adds, "I was swept off my feet by Mackers from the first day. It was a beautiful thing. It wasn't about color. It was everybody, a family event, all the players in a beautiful atmosphere and environment having fun."[4]

Magic Johnson's All-Stars

In November, 1991, Magic Johnson, one of the most beloved athletes of all time, made a stunning announcement. He had been diagnosed with the HIV virus. As a whole, Americans did not handle the HIV/AIDS epidemic of the 1980s and 1990s very well, and Magic was a victim of this. He lost the adulation of numerous fans and quite a few gave him a short time to live. Worse yet was the response by some of his colleagues, who expressed their discomfort at the idea of being on the same court with him. Some players even questioned his sexuality.

For a while Magic left basketball completely. But he would return in glorious fashion. On February 9, 1992, after being away from the league for three months, Johnson played in the NBA All-Star Game, scoring twenty-five points and winning the MVP award, while hitting a huge shot at the end of the half. In the 1992 Summer Olympics, Johnson played on the original "Dream Team," considered to be the greatest team ever assembled. That fall Johnson announced in a press conference his plans to return to the Lakers for the 1992-1993 season. However, during the pre-season, Johnson was deeply hurt by the negative reaction from some of the players towards his virus. He decided to retire before the season began.

Though feeling unwelcome in the NBA, Magic still yearned to play the game he loved. He formed the Magic Johnson All-Stars, a barnstorming team to be composed of former NBA and college players. Magic's All-Stars would tour the country playing against teams from the CBA. In addition, they entertained fans around the world playing exhibition games overseas. Joining the team were former pros, such as Mark Aguirre, Reggie Theus, John Long, Earl Cureton, Jim Farmer, and Lester Conner.

Bobbie learned that the Magic Johnson All-Stars would be playing Grand Rapids' CBA team, the "Hoops." He imagined a nice Valentine's present from Magic to Sugar's hometown fans. For Sugar to suit up with the Magic Johnson All-Stars against the Hoops. The game was scheduled to take place on February 14, 1993. As Bobbie said, "Just once more around the block in the old neighborhood."[5]

When Magic heard of Bobbie's request, he said, "I should have thought about him in the first place." Both Michiganders, Sugar and Magic knew of each other and had played together in pick-up games and tournaments over the years. In addition, while at Central Michigan, Sugar had been a camp counselor for Dr. Charles Tucker, Magic's long-time advisor, at Dr. Tucker's Basketball Camp. Magic introduced Sugar to the campers as the greatest shooter in the country. Isiah Thomas was also working at the camp and the campers begged Isiah to take Sugar on in a one-on-one contest. Isiah wisely refused.

After hearing from Bobbie, Magic let Dale Beard, a friend in Michigan, know that he wanted to reach Sugar. After a pick-up game together, Beard told Sugar that Magic was putting together an all-star team and wanted him on the team. As Sugar recounts, "He gave me the phone number of Magic's agent at the time, Lon Rosen. I called Rosen, and said, 'Tell Magic that Sugar Mel wants to play on your team.' Within the hour, Magic calls, saying, 'Come on and try out like everybody else.' And I said, 'Cool, I'll be there!'"

To get ready for the tryout and earn a spot on the 12-man roster, Sugar trained harder than ever. Already a well-conditioned athlete, he showed up for Magic's camp in his best shape ever. Though at thirty-three years old he was considered past his prime, he grinned. "I came into camp in better shape than anyone except for Magic."[6]

As a result, Sugar was well-prepared to raise the level of his game to match the camp's high intensity. Magic ran camp as if they were trying out for the NBA. Anyone unwilling to pay the price would not have the right to suit up for his All-Star team.

Others trying out with Sugar were Reggie Theus, Greg Foster, Mike McGee, Grant Long, Earl Cureton, Jack Haley, John Long, and Gregory Kelser. At first Sugar tried to blend in by distributing the basketball. But after Sugar hit several long-range jumpers in a row, Magic stopped the game and reprimanded him. "Look, your role on this team is to shoot the ball and my role is to get you the ball!"

He was in his element. "I got in a zone," Sugar says. "I shot the ball pretty well, so they started calling me, 'Radar'."[7]

Players began asking him what team(s) he had played for and why they hadn't heard of him before. Other players, such as Theus, McGee, and Foster, rubbed their eyes in amazement. Reflecting on how his brother rose to the challenge and proved that he belonged on Magic's All-Star Team, Bobbie choked up. "After all these years, it justified my faith in him. I always knew that he could play at this level, but he just didn't get the chance. He'd come down and put one up from way out there and nail it, and people would say, 'Who is this guy?' Magic would laugh and say, 'He's my homeboy,' and make sure he got the ball again."[8]

Sugar even outdid the others in one-on-one matches, Bobbie said. "Every day they have one-on-one pool play, and by the end of the week, Melvin had won his bracket and Magic had won the other."[9]

After the tryout, Magic congratulated Sugar for making the team. He added, "I didn't know that you were going to do as well as you did and be in the kind of shape you're in. You proved me wrong."

The two greatest smiles in Michigan basketball brought even more smiles to those who watched them play together. As Magic, arguably the greatest play-maker in the history of the game, teamed up with Sugar, arguably the greatest long-range shooter in the history of the game.

Area All-Star Teams

Playing for Magic's All-Star Team in Los Angeles gave Sugar the idea to start his own all-star team. "I can do something like that back here," he realized. "I know a lot of guys who still love the game." Through his connections in basketball, Sugar formed a nucleus of stars in the Grand Rapids area. They committed to play exhibition games against local colleges, pro-amateur teams, and similar All-Star squads. Some players on Sugar's All-Star teams include Lacey James, Michael "Pops" Simms, Reggie Green, Bobby Taylor, Roosevelt Pritchett, Barry Fordham, Ben Poquette, and Sugar's nephew Eric. Just as in high school and college, Sugar would leave behind a highlight film's worth of memories. That reel validates his reputation and the team's chosen name to all who watched.

With the advantage of the three-point rule, Sugar at last was in his own element. If his Sugar Mel's All-Stars were down at the half, they stepped up their defense for a comeback to win. On the offensive end of the court, Sugar would hit threes left and right. Anthony Gordon was one of Sugar's All-Stars. He explains,

 I think the three-pointer inspired Sugar to continue to play even more. His style of play was so suited to the three-point play. We won games often because we had a three-pointer. No one on

the floor could shoot the three as good as him. We figured if we just locked on defense, we could contend.

Years earlier, Sugar had played an alumni game against his alma mater during "Thunder" Dan Majerle's senior year in 1987-1988. Some Central Michigan players had heard about Sugar, but had never seen him play before. Dave Ginsberg says, "He came in and put on a show. He was probably around 27 or 28, so he was really at his peak. People came early to see that game, though it was just an alumni game. Melvin's a short six foot...but he knew how to create space with the dribble, so you couldn't get to his shot. It was phenomenal."

In Flint, a pipeline for some of the state's greatest players, Sugar took on three-time NBA All-Star Glen Rice and several other NBA players. During a shoot-out, Sugar nailed 63 points and Rice 60. Then at age 38, Sugar would out-duel another legendary Flint player, Michigan State's Mateen Cleaves. Cleaves had just won the Big Ten Player of the Year Award for the second year in a row in 1999. He was on his way to lead the Spartans to the National Championship in 2000. Sugar, however, left Cleaves in his tracks, scoring fifty-five points. Mateen was completely embarrassed in front of his hometown fans. All he could do was to imitate "the Michael Jordan shrug" to express his exasperation. Mateen fouled out of the game in his desperate attempt to stop Sugar.

In addition to playing for his own All-Star team, Sugar was recruited by former Zeeland High School and Aquinas College star Chuck Berghorst (1992). Berghorst wanted Sugar for his and his dad's team, "Team Berghorst and Sons" in the 1990s through 2000. After graduating from Aquinas, Chuck took over the team. He recruited some of the better local players to join him in playing in tournaments all over the Midwest. The team would play with and against various Michigan stars, including

Glen Rice, Steve Scheffler, Andre Rison, Jeff Grayer, Johnny Dawkins, and Duane Washington. According to Chuck's dad, Ford, "I saw Sugar play against NBA guys and he was just as good as some of the best players in the league."

Proving that he hadn't lost his touch on the verge of the new millennium, in August of 2000, at the age of forty, Sugar set the Holland Recreation League record. He had sixty-eight points, scoring 28 three-pointers in the process, some over two feet beyond the NBA three-point line.[10] Sugar continues to defy his age wherever he plays. Ginsberg exults, "He is just so good. Somebody said he was playing in an over fifty-five-years-old game and he scored sixty points."

Though he doesn't have "Played in the NBA" on his resumé, Sugar's post-collegiate career more than validates his candidacy as one of the greatest long-distance shooters in the history of the game. The player Magic Johnson nicknamed Radar may have played under the radar in hot, sweaty gyms with limited seating capacity. But those who saw him play understand Bennette Gay's boast, that Sugar is the best player to have never played in the NBA.

Sugar mulls over old newspaper clippings of some of post-collegiate games. He marvels,

 I'm even tripping on these numbers, using the three-point shot. These are important factors in my playing career that people probably don't know. If I'd had the fair chance to display my God-given shooting abilities at the NBA level, they would have seen something phenomenal.

Mentor of the Game

Sugar's regrets do not defeat him. In the gyms and playgrounds of Grand Rapids, Sugar continues to excel. From pros to elementary kids learning how to shoot a lay-up, he shares his expertise.

One professional to benefit from his mentorship was Loy Vaught. He starred for East Kentwood High School and helped the University of Michigan Wolverines win the 1989 NCAA Men's Division I Basketball Championship. Vaught played most of his NBA career for the Los Angeles Clippers. Fellow East Kentwood High School grad, Anthony Gordon, witnessed the 6'9" Vaught and the 6'1" Sugar battle. Sugar sought to prepare Vaught for the rigors of the NBA, while getting himself ready for his touring team. Gordon says,

Melvin challenged Loy in a one-on-one contest. In his seventh or eighth year in the NBA, Loy probably should have been on the All-Star team. He led the Clippers in scoring and rebounding for three or four years. On top of that, Melvin was in his late 30s. Loy thought, "No problem," given his height advantage and youth.

Gordon goes on to describe,

 All the other players stop to watch them play, as they're going back and forth. Melvin hangs in there by doing all these trick shots and using a lot of head fakes. They're talking trash to each other. Sure enough, they battle it out down to game point with Melvin having the ball. He drives down the lane, Loy trying to stop him from scoring. He twists, turns, then dribbles to the middle of the lane and throws up a drop hook on Loy. While the ball is in the air, Mel says to Loy, "Ball Game!" and the ball drops into the basket.

After serving as a missionary overseas for several years, I returned to Grand Rapids. There I witnessed Sugar challenge an aspiring middle schooler to a shooting match at the MVP

club at Cascade. From the sidelines, I saw Sugar interrupt their match to demonstrate how to hold the ball and follow through after releasing a shot. I've been told by others that it's not uncommon for Sugar to befriend players on the courts and playgrounds of Grand Rapids. He cannot help but offer his sage advice on how they might improve their game. He loves people and loves to help. It is a winning combination.

Over a recent Christmas break at MVP, at fifty-nine years old, Sugar played non-stop for six straight hours without a break. Local high school and college players vied to dethrone him as the "King of Grand Rapids Basketball." Instead, Sugar continued to reign on the playing floor, in spite of having to ice his sore knees in the locker room afterward.

A few months later, in an eye-popping shooting exhibition, he made 53 shots in a row from well beyond three-point range. Symbolically, the numbers 59 and 53 serve as reminders that Sugar isn't past his prime, yet. In the case of the latter number, though, he might have made even more than 53. A phone call from his feeder's wife interrupted Sugar's streak. Aquinas College's assistant woman's basketball Coach Austin Randel needed to feed himself and go home for dinner.

Given his off-the-charts basketball IQ, his love for the game, and his approachable demeanor, Sugar could make an ideal basketball coach. However, Sugar has never been interested in coaching full-time. He'd much rather play the game than sit on the side watching others play. In addition, it's nearly impossible to instill in others the same passion for the game of basketball that he has. Moreover, Sugar's friendly and calm disposition doesn't fit the profile of a head coach.

Bob Becker conjectures, "He might be a great coach, but his personality was not throwing down a clipboard and yelling, 'How many times have I told you to do this?' I don't see that in Melvin. He'd be like, 'That's the twelfth time you've double dribbled, but that's all right. We'll work on it.'"

He might not see himself as a coach, but one summer, he was helping out at Bennette Gay's basketball camp when Gay coached at Central High School. Bennette says, "He really enjoyed it. He started doing the camp and fell in love with it." After that, the idea for having his own basketball camp took off. Sugar never forgot that his family couldn't afford to send him to basketball camp as a kid. That season, Sugar and his brother Bobbie expedited the idea to offer an affordable basketball camp for the kids in Grand Rapids.

Bobbie points to his brother. "He pushed me to get this thing started back in the day. He wanted to give back to the community. A good way to start was creating an affordable basketball camp for the area kids. The results have been great —phenomenal."

Bennette nods. "Giving back to the kids. That's Melvin, what he's doing now. He's got a big heart."

21

SWEET SHOT GIVES BACK TO THE COMMUNITY

> He's a credit to his community and has had an unbelievably positive influence on so many lives in this area. Look at the kids he's been touching through this camp. He's been reaching out and putting his hand on the backs of a whole bunch of kids showing them the right way to go.
>
> — BOB BECKER

The newest spin on Mel's dream officially began in 1993 with a week-long camp. Then dubbed the First Annual Melvin "Sugar" McLaughlin All-Star Boys Basketball Camp for inner-city youth, it was hosted at Ottawa Hills from July 19-23.

And it started out with a bang (or more accurately, Thunder), when Traverse City native and CMU star Dan Majerle came into town to help out, fresh after facing Michael Jordan and his Bulls in the NBA finals.

"Thunder" Dan Majerle's presence added legitimacy to the camp. After the camp. the two leading scorers from Central

Michigan would team up together in a post-camp All-Star game. The game is still talked about to this day.

Before camp even ended at 5 p.m., crowds lined up outside of Ottawa Hills High School at 4 o'clock for the 7 o'clock tip off. An estimated 2,200 fans packed the gym; hundreds were turned away due to fire code regulations.

Witnesses will never forget the legendary game. Many contend that such a talent level has never been seen before or since on the same playing floor at the same time in Grand Rapids. Not even at the TA-WA-SI games.

NBA All-Star Dan Majerle launched 10 three-pointers for 37 points, earning the game's Most Valuable Player. Sugar bombed in 28 points, and another CMU great "Big Ben" Poquette added 20 points to lead Team Purple to a 164-158 win over Team White. Dave Ginsberg coached the squad to victory.

Additional firepower for the Purple included David Tuck (Ferris State) with 22 points, 18 from Carlton Valentine (MSU), 12 from Damon Patterson (Kalamazoo/Oklahoma University), and 10 points each from Steve Honderd (Calvin College) and "Jumping" Jack Kelly (Creston High).

They weren't facing a bunch of stooges, either. With Coach Granville Brown, Grand Rapids Hoops' star Reggie Fox led Team White at 38 points. Michigan State's Gregory "Special K" Kelser had 32 points. Mark Hughes (Muskegon Reeths-Puffer/Detroit Pistons, 23 points), Mike McCall (Ottawa Hills/Oklahoma City College) added 20, Reggie Green (Ottawa Hills/Youngstown State), and Charlie Mandt (Grand Valley State) added 14.[1]

Although Sugar's basketball camp started out with Thunder, it faced some storms in its early years. Some years lack of support forced a brief hiatus. Initially, the camp was held over five days. But the camp's high intensity wore out both campers and staff members by the week's end. They shortened the camp to the current three days. Being pushed to greatness, though, can still give campers fatigue and sore muscles! By the third day of camp, it's like Easter Sunday in August. Everyone greets each other with renewed enthusiasm, and depart on a high note with eager anticipation of applying the lessons learned. The players leave the camp, never the same again.

For two years in a row I've personally observed Sugar's camp. I can attest that it's unique to any basketball camp I've ever been part of. When it comes to basketball, the camp is exceptional. Bobbie and Sugar lead their like-minded staff members to strive for greatness as a team. The staff objective of helping each camper succeed both on the court and off the court is beautiful to witness.

What I find most outstanding, however, is how the community of Grand Rapids rallies around Sugar in supporting his camp. Most basketball camps consist primarily of the campers and their counselors, along with some featured guests. Sugar's family is so important to him, his camp is more on par with a three-day family reunion. In fact, because so many McLaughlins participate in camp, their annual family reunion shifted from Christmas to follow the camp.

People from all walks of life gather together to support Sugar's camp. Because of them, he is able to boast, "Sugar Mel's All-Star Basketball Camp is the oldest, affordable camp in Grand Rapids. Praise God!" If campers show up hungry, Sugar sends them off to grab a breakfast provided by their sponsors. Every message sent to the campers is, "We care about you. You are why we are here."

Some play a direct role in the camp in working with the kids. Bobbie serves as camp director. His son Quinn and his sister Patricia's son Nick also contribute. Coaches and former area players add to the mix. These include Bennette Gay, Anthony Gordon, Steve "Preacher" Lee, Robert Roelofs, Mike Noble, and twin sisters Kamau and Brianne Day. Just like a winning basketball team works together to accomplish their goals, these volunteers are a team. They all team up in offering their time, expertise, energy, and enthusiasm towards making the camp a sweet success for all the campers no matter their age or playing ability.

Dave Ginsberg customarily makes an appearance. His moving motivational speeches no doubt stay in the hearts and minds of the campers long after their playing days end. Along with that, church members, school volunteers, and family members help out behind the scenes. They pitch in whenever needed. They get ice for an injured player, carry sports drinks up the steps, take pictures, and offer encouragement to tired campers. They have been drawn to what God is doing through Sugar's camp in touching lives in the community. Sugar challenges the campers to dare to be great rather than settle for anything less. Motivated to do all they can to make this three-day camp the greatest experience possible for all involved, these assistants refuse to settle for less.

During the three-day camp, it's like an episode of the old television show, *This is Your Life*. Numerous community members stop by, grateful for Sugar and his extraordinary job of impacting futures through Sweet Shot camp. They've not only assisted Sugar in becoming the area's best basketball player of all time, but more importantly, have contributed to his becoming a highly respected role model. It does, indeed, take a village. And the village—and the villagers—all win.

Mel Atkins, Sugar's middle school coach, and Jim Haskins, his high school coach, appear. During a break in the action, Sugar hugs each man, in appreciation for their presence at camp and all the ways they have contributed to his life.

Among the sponsors of the camp are Johnny Brann, owner of Brann's Steakhouse & Grille; Joe Lavoi, general manager of Grand Rapids' Fox Motors; and Augie Vitale, owner of Vitale's Pizza chain. They stop by to check how things are going, and how they might further support the camp.

Michael Zoerhoff, Superintendent of the East Kentwood School District, swings in to watch the camp's progress. In addition, local media members, such as Bob Becker, former sports editor of *The Grand Rapids Press*, and Steve Kaminski, sports writer for *The Grand Rapids Press* and MLive.com, greet Sugar and Bobbie like old friends.

One of the remaining living Grand Rapids Tackers, Clarence Carlisle, watches proudly. Sugar passes the baton of playing skills and life's advice to the area's youth, and Carlisle beams. Mel is continuing the Tackers' legacy they had bequeathed Sugar in his childhood. Former Tacker Herschel Turner's health prevents him from attending the camp. Still, his thoughts and prayers remain with one of the most visible fruits of his labors, from his days as the leader of the Baxter Community Center.

Johnny Walker gave Sugar his first job maintaining the courts of King Park and getting his daily shots in. Walker and sidekicks Rex Jones, Michael Timms, and Jimmy Carter, have changed lives in the community through sports. They watch with gratification from the sidelines. Sugar has picked up the mantle they have passed down to him. He's using basketball to reach out to the next generation.

One summer when I visited Sugar's camp, an impromptu mini East Grand Rapids reunion even took place. Johnny Lui, whose dad owned the Hong Kong Inn Chinese Restaurant, was the oldest son of one of the first immigrant families to attend East. He now serves as an interventionist at East Kentwood High School and volunteers at the camp. Johnny Brann, one of the sponsors, attended East with my older brothers. He appeared for an interview. Former East football star Corey Smith, one of the few black students at East when I attended and was several grades behind me, showed up to support the kids. And my best friend from elementary school, Brian Gilmore, attended camp from Washington State with his daughter, Emma, shooting film for a documentary we are creating about Sugar. The last time I saw Brian was at our graduation party at his dad's farm in 1982!

Things have changed a bit in recent years, but when we attended East, it didn't matter what your traditional rival was, everyone had one thing in common. They hated East Grand Rapids! But there at camp, we swapped old Eastie stories and memories of classmates and teachers, as fellow alumni of the most hated schools in the area at the gym of our biggest rival school in the former OK Red Conference, East Kentwood High School. Only in this case, we've been united together not in hate but in our common love for Sugar!

Hebrews 12:1 says, "We are surrounded by a cloud of witnesses." My throat tightens as I survey the beaming faces surrounding the gym, Sugar, and his camp. As Michael Timms said to me over and over during one camp, "Melvin is an even better person than player. There are not a lot of people I can say that about."

Glenn VanWieren is a retired basketball coach of Hope College in Holland, Michigan. He says, "Sugar's always giving back to the community through the gift of basketball. God gave him a special gift that he's been able to use wisely."

Along with the visible witnesses on the sidelines, invisible witnesses have gone to heaven before Sugar. He will never forget the role of his parents, Bobbie Sr. and Mary Ruth, and his older sisters Patricia and Gracie. Numerous uncles and aunts, including Uncle Ollie and Aunt Ruth, and Uncle Maxie and Aunt Venie, shaped him. The music of their lives continues to reverberate through him and this extended camp family.

Sugar smiles his brilliant crescent smile, and demonstrates how to make a bank shot that Don "The Animal" Edwards first taught him. Besides Edwards, other former Tackers who have died come to mind. Even the camp's name, Sugar Mel, stirs up memories of George Knighton, who nicknamed him in elemen-

216 | REV. DR. VERNON E. WENDT, JR.

tary school. The late Ernie Johnson's son, Arian, pay his respects every summer. As he huddles with the campers, he recalls doing the same with former teammate Kim Thompson.

As Sugar catches Linda's gaze at the registration table, he remembers Anthony Winston. He owes a lot to his former teammate and friend, who introduced them in high school. His face lights up even more to see daughter Morgan helping out, and when his son, Melvin, shows up with his beautiful grand-daughters in tow. Though his older sisters, Patricia and Gracie, are not visibly present, their children play significant parts in the camp.

For the little boy who lost his mother at such a tender age, this camp is a dream come true, a family. Kids, their parents, and grandparents gather around to encourage not only their own kids but the other players, coaches, and one another. Sugar goes out of his way to befriend every kid at the camp, exchanging phone numbers. In his encouraging, warm voice, he says, "I'll be watching for you in the upcoming season." He challenges campers by name to be great on and off the court.

Far from being an aloof superstar, his humble and inviting personality makes everyone feel like they're his friend. He might be physically exhausted at the end of these three long days, but he's just as enthusiastic when the camp ends as he was in the beginning. He is, in fact, exultant. "I'm just thankful to God to give back to the community! That's what it's all about!"

Infirmities sideline most of the Grand Rapids' athletic veterans who gather at his camp. Someday it might be Sugar watching on the sidelines. I witness yet another three-pointer sink into the bucket and laugh out loud. There appears to be nothing in the way to slow him down as he approaches his sixtieth birthday.

A prophet may not be accepted in his hometown. But there's a sweet-shooting basketball player known as Sugar, who is the "toast of the town" in "Beer City, USA" (aka Grand Rapids, Michigan). Over and over at Sugar Mel's Sweet Shot Camp, people express variations of, "This is what the news should be covering on TV!" "This is the best thing Sugar could have done!"

As Bennette Gay remarks, "Through this camp, the kids in Grand Rapids get to know someone special, not just as a player but as a person."

Rather than uprooting to a more glamorous city with nicer weather, Sugar is content to bloom where God transplanted him as an eight-year-old. In 2009, he was even featured on a track titled "Swishas and Dosha," penned by William Jackson (aka "Willie da Kid"). In the song, Willie da Kid boasts about playing basketball in Grand Rapids like Melvin McLaughlin.[2] And Sugar Mel T-shirts, hats, and medallions are popular fashion items among the youth in GR.

The city's all-time greatest basketball player is one of the most beloved and popular figures in West Michigan. Sugar will never forget all those who gave of themselves to help him be the person and role model he has become.

What a great privilege: playing the game of basketball, then using this gift as a platform to give back to the community. Sugar knows, and gives God all the glory and honor.

22

THE RE-BIRTH OF A DREAM

66 Shoot for the moon. If you miss it you will land
among the stars.

— LES BROWN

Why wasn't one of the greatest long-range shooters
in the history of the game given a fair chance
when he tried out professionally?

Perhaps, it was lack of exposure? Granted, some NBA
players were Grand Rapids products (e.g., Loy Vaught, Chris
Kaman, Ben Handlogten, Matt Steigenga, Steve Scheffler, and
Devin Booker). And Central Michigan has certainly produced
its share of NBA players (e.g., Nate Hoffman, Chris Kaman, Ben
Kelso, Dan Majerle, Jim McElroy, Ben Poquette, and Dan
Roundfield). Plus, a number of NBA players didn't qualify for
post-season play in their collegiate careers. Nonetheless,
Melvin Sugar McLaughlin wasn't exactly a household name
when he tried out for the league.

Or maybe Sugar was overlooked by the NBA teams because
of his slight body build. Dave Ginsberg says, "If he would have

been two inches taller and 20 pounds heavier of muscle, he probably would have gotten in the league. When he got in, it was just the wrong timing. The way the game is played today would have been much more conducive to his making it, because people want to see entertainment."

Former Pistons' coach Ray Scott adds, "Teams look for someone whose body will hold up to the rigors of the NBA grind. That's a minimum of 100 games, if you include play-offs. Melvin didn't appear to fit the NBA prototype."

Yet, Sugar was more than capable of competing in the league. In spite of all the defensive pressure against him throughout his career, he was tireless and practically injury free. Jim Haskins insists that his former Creston prodigy would have only gotten stronger in the NBA, given his work ethic and motivation. Jimmy Boylen contends, "I judge my players by their heart not by their size. Sugar had the heart to compete against anyone in the league."

Plenty of players have made the NBA with a similar body frame as Sugar's (e.g., 6'0" 150 lbs. Elliot Perry; 6'1" 150 lbs. "Tiny" Nate Archibald; 5'10" 152 lbs. Tyrus Edney; 5'11" 153 lbs. Stan Kimborough; 6'1" 160 lbs. Dee Brown; and 6'1" 165 lbs. Allan Iverson). Anthony Gordon likens Sugar's athleticism and quickness to Iverson's, except for Iverson's dunking skills. Although Sonny Newman counters that Sugar was a far better shooter than AI ever was. Given his shooting range, speed, knowledge of the game, and tenacity, Sugar could have more than made up for his lack of size.

But the NBA is a numbers' game. Players with guaranteed contracts and higher round draft picks leave little room for lower round and unrecognized players like Sugar. He may have outplayed the other players in the Pistons' camp, but it was nearly impossible for him to crack the hardened shell of the Piston staff and their predetermined lineup.

In today's league, he would have certainly found a place

due to shooting range and ability alone. However, in the case of the Pistons, incoming coach Chuck Daly wanted mostly rough and tumble defensive players, when Sugar tried out for the team. The players making this cut would eventually form the nucleus of his back-to-back NBA Championship teams in 1988-1989 and 1989-1990. They were notorious for their physical and aggressive style of play. Sugar didn't fit the team's Bad Boys gladiator approach to the game when he tried out.

When so-called experts witnessed Sugar shooting the lights out, over and against the outreached hands of frustrated defenders, maybe they considered it a fluke rather than a pattern, especially given his size. If so, sideline watchers figured he couldn't possibly keep up the current scoring pace throughout a regular NBA season. He has disproven skeptics and doubters, convincing them of his astonishing shooting prowess his entire career.

Speculations remain just that: speculations. They could also become reasons for bitterness, second-guessing, and an entire loss of heart. Not for Sugar, however. For almost his entire life, his faith in God has informed his character, his actions, and his attitude. He trusts God's reasons and purposes for blocking the NBA attempts.

The guy who rebounded his own missed shots, chose to rebound from his greatest disappointment. He was unstoppable on the court, and so is his certainty that the long shot of his life is an offering to God. Offering up his talent for basketball to God for His glory is his only option and his first choice.

Was this easy? No. Accepting that his dream had not come to fruition the way he expected took time. Though the cut was years ago, I still heard the hurt in his voice, when he said,

 Basketball has been such a big part of my life. From a human perspective, I still get frustrated. I know how much I love the game. And how much

work I put into fulfilling my dream, only to not play in the NBA. And to have things happen the way they did. It's easy to ask, "Why me?" After success at all these levels, I get to this optimal level, at my ultimate goal, my ultimate dream. And they're shutting the doors on me? Why? I've proven that I can play on this level, but people ignored me and turned their backs on me. It was very frustrating and very, very discouraging.

Rather than the human perspective, Sugar chooses a lens of faith. This has been his viewfinder since receiving Christ as a child. He had to choose to come closer to the Lord as a result of this, rather than turn away from God. Growing older, he says, "I had to rely on God more and more during the ups and downs. Look for Him to revive me, recover me, give me a positive attitude about life and what I'm doing."

Perhaps these were tests, he acknowledges now. "How much do you really believe in Me?" God's answer reassures him daily: "I got your back no matter what."

Acceptance is a choice, and he's chosen to accept that his heavenly Father has a plan other than NBA stardom in giving him this special gift. Those wounds are healing to become battle scars of victory.

One possible reason Sugar humbly acknowledges is that perhaps he wasn't ready to deal with the pitfalls of being an NBA player. Fame and fortune have led to the downfall of many gifted players. "Maybe God thought if I got to that level, I'd ruin everything He planned, because I couldn't handle the NBA lifestyle. Some players spent all their money, became drug addicts, or died in a car crash. A lot of players who played in the NBA and made a lot of money, are not living as good a life as we are right now."

His brother Bobbie had thrown a basketball at his chest to

prevent him from potentially being hit by a car when he was four. Perhaps, God knocked the wind out of his NBA dream in order to keep him from experiencing a potential disaster. Thankfully, the basketball to the chest didn't deter his love and passion for the game. Nor did being cut from the NBA. Instead, he continues to recognize basketball as a gift to him from God for His purposes.

Throughout the Bible we find other examples of people who had an idea, plan, dream, or goal that was dead to them. But God supernaturally intervened. Not only did He resurrect it, He fulfilled it in a way far beyond their dreams. (Consider Abraham, Joseph, Moses, and ultimately Jesus Himself.) Ephesians 3:20 describes, "Now to him who is able to do immeasurably more than all we ask or imagine, according to his power."

Correspondingly, there are several reasons why God may have allowed Sugar's dream of being an NBA star to turn out differently than he anticipated.

First, and foremost, God wants us to put Him above all else. When our lives don't turn out the way we expect, where else can we turn, but to God? In spite of disappointment, Sugar has learned to put God first in his life above all else. He says,

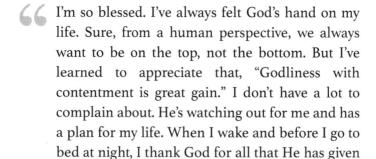

> I'm so blessed. I've always felt God's hand on my life. Sure, from a human perspective, we always want to be on the top, not the bottom. But I've learned to appreciate that, "Godliness with contentment is great gain." I don't have a lot to complain about. He's watching out for me and has a plan for my life. When I wake and before I go to bed at night, I thank God for all that He has given me.

Perhaps God allows our life's dreams to be broken, to test

our faith: do we really trust Him as we say we do? First Peter 1:6-7 tells us, "In all this you greatly rejoice, though now for a little while you may have had to suffer grief in all kinds of trials. These have come so that the proven genuineness of your faith —of greater worth than gold, which perishes even though refined by fire—may result in praise, glory and honor when Jesus Christ is revealed."

As I've gotten to know Sugar, hearing from him about his basketball career, his faith in God has clearly been proven genuine.

Because of his faith, along with the support of his family, friends and community members, Sugar has successfully rebounded from disappointment. And he's made a slam dunk by reaching out to the community of Grand Rapids. God has transformed his bitter experience into something sweeter than he could have imagined. As Bobbie explains, "God blessed my brother in His way, not our way. Realistically, he's probably more popular now than when he was playing. God is using him to reach out to these kids through his camps and work in the community. That's why he's being blessed so much at this current time." He goes on,

> The world missed out on seeing Sugar Mel, but we didn't. I thank God for that. But God said, "It ain't about the world. It's about me! This is what I want Sugar to do for Me! Right here, I want Sugar to inspire people. I want Sugar to inspire these kids. I want Sugar to lead. Now I'm going to give him his props, but it's going to be my way, not Sugar's way, not the world's way."

Sugar Mel may not be a household name with some of the kids in Grand Rapids. They know other basketball greats, though: Lebron James, Kobe Bryant, and Michael Jordan. But stories are generational. Bobbie says, "When campers' parents and grandparents tell them stories of what they saw, they get a better understanding of Sugar Mel. That's why the camp is growing and getting so popular. The kids may not have seen him play, but what they're hearing about him is so amazing, they know he must have been something special."

Sugar's face illuminates. "Giving back is really what it's all about!" Of his legacy, he says,

 I want to be remembered for more than just being a basketball player. I want to be remembered for who I am as a person, how I treated others, and how I tried to be tactful, inspiring and motivating. No matter how much money you have or don't have, what else you have or what you don't have. I'm going to treat everybody the same: with love, thoughtfulness, and consideration. I don't care who you are. Above all, I want to be known as a loving, God-fearing person who was interested in trying to help people. That's more important to me than all the money in the world or a fleet of cars. Eventually, you'll have to leave all that behind.

When Sugar is summoned to his heavenly home, he will not just be remembered as a phenomenal basketball player. More importantly, he will be remembered for the many lives influenced by his "sweeter than Sugar" personality and outstanding character.

That is certainly his long-term earthly reputation. Without exception, when I brought up his name in conversations and interviews for this book, people responded with joy and fondness. Recalling a sweet-shooting guard nicknamed Sugar still moved them to amazement.

Throughout his lifetime, Sugar has sweetened a lot of lives in the midst of an often sinful and bitter world. God has raised him up in this generation to let his light shine on the playing floor. But more than that, all around the various neighborhoods of Grand Rapids and beyond.

23

SWEET DREAMS!

> Ultimately, our dreams are not about us, about us making money or a name for ourselves. Though neither is bad, both are shortsighted. We don't want to shortchange what God can do. Our dreams, inspired and gifted by God, become the means for God making a difference in this world.
>
> — JANE RUBIETTA, *FINDING YOUR DREAM*

I magine if we all viewed our particular skills and talents as a special gift from God, used to mold and shape our faith and character, as well as our witness to others. In nearly every interview I read or did with him, Sugar inevitably gave thanks to God for his ability to play the game. I contend that this dedication of his gifts to God made all the difference. Instead of being just a good player, he became a great player. His faith was instrumental in a successful rebound after the death of a lifelong dream.

In the Bible, a few of Jesus' followers got a glimpse of heaven at his transfiguration. His body became radiant with light, alongside Moses and Elijah. God was reminding Jesus' trainees of the Big Picture. When they witnessed Jesus endure his sufferings and death on the cross, they were not to despair. In spite of how bad things appeared, in the end everything would turn out all right. One day, they would behold Jesus in his glorified body.

Correspondingly, Sugar has helped me glimpse heaven in the way he shined on the basketball court. Though I barely knew him at the time, I knew he was one of a kind. Not only in his formidable ability to shoot the ball, but the manner in which he played. Bob Becker remarks, "He just made basketball fun." Even more, by giving us all a glimpse of heaven, Sugar serves as a bright light in many lives, in the midst of dark times.

For Sugar, basketball has been a means of survival from the wracking grief of his mother's death, and then his sister's. That orange ball, a hoop, and a hard surface created a sanctuary for recovery. Every swish, every bounce, every rebound worked even beyond healing from grief. Shot after shot, he honed his focus, discipline, and personal growth. In the process, he developed a gift that would do more than see him through the educational dreams his mother whispered to Bobbie as she lay dying. It would ultimately provide a future for countless eager kids. Kids like him, kids needing hope, a mentor, guidance, and someone to simply believe in them.

In no sense is recovery from the death of a dream simple or even final. Long after the list is posted and the players either empty their lockers or move into them, the what-ifs will continue. What if I'd done this, or someone else had done that, or...?

But, as Sugar says, that's not helpful. Instead, figure out the next shot, get into position for the next assist, regardless of the game. Whether in life or in basketball, the principle is the same. Keep your eye on the goal, don't let the last mistake mess up your next shot. And keep shooting.

From his earliest days, Sugar's God Thing helped him redirect after every disappointment and loss. The certainty that the One who saved his life that day in traffic wanted him to help others never left him. As he traveled across the country, the fire inside refused to die. He could only think, he says, "of the kids back home, and how I wanted to help them have good lives."

The rebirth of the basketball dream, shifting from the NBA to the Midwestern hardwoods, became the sweetest dream— not just for a kid nicknamed Sugar. His basketball long shot offers kids the sweetest shot ever: the chance to focus, hone, learn, and grow. The chance, Sugar says, to succeed. Through it all, Sugar hopes his life and his work will point people to the same God. The One who gave him the gift of a pebble-surfaced ball and the courage to keep launching toward the goal.

On an encouraging note, Sugar Mel's Sweet Shot Basketball Camp ends. Sugar, Bobbie, and several others are scheduled to shoot baskets at King Park for photos. Arriving early, I tell some kids who are there for an organized game, "Sugar is going to be here soon. Do you want to be in a photo shoot?"

They squint at me, puzzled. "Who's Sugar?"

"Just the greatest shooter I've ever seen. He used to practically live at this park, while perfecting his shot."

Their coach appears and confirms my boast. Serendipitously, he tells the kids, "Sugar taught me how to really play the game of basketball when I was younger."

Soon, Bobbie, Sugar and his son Pooh, Anthony Gordon and our photographer show up. Finally, I get to match a few shots with my basketball hero, managing a few 25-feet shots of my own.

In his aviator sunglasses, Sugar gazes around the park. The image mirrored in his glasses reflects the court's emptiness. A lone player leaps up for a shot. "The Chief" flashes his well-known smile, then turns wistful. "When I was growing up, on a beautiful Saturday morning like today, players would be lined up all over the park for a chance to play."

Instead, other than the kids I talked to earlier waiting for an organized game on the main court, scarcely any other players surround us. Times have changed. Playground basketball is not what it used to be.

Grand Rapids' greatest player of all time looks around the park again, and says to Bobbie, "Hey, they moved the courts! They used to be further south of the park."

His big brother shakes his head. Anthony joins in. "No, man, you got 'Old-timers' disease."

Then again, they decide, who would know better than Sugar? This was his home-away-from-home. Bobbie points to the nylon nets, hanging threadbare and desperate. "They replaced the chain nets for this? Who's working at the park these days?"

We all gape at the rims. Sugar would have traded these worn-out nets in a heartbeat.

In spite of the tattered mesh, Sugar begins to sink jumper after jumper. "This is real basketball. Outdoors. Never mind the conditions. This is where shooters are made."

Sweating from the summer sun, a mini-workout, and the photos on the hot court, we leave the park and walk up the street to their former house on Prince Street. How appropriate, I think, to have Prince Street just up the road from King Park. The house is well-kept, the driveway still steep, the grass trimmed. I wonder if the current occupants know what stories line the walls of that home?

Bobbie and Sugar reminisce about their years on Prince Street: the crowded dinner table, the gospel music filling the home on Sundays. We can almost hear the laughter, the singing, the rambunctious play of a houseful of kids. In our minds, the unlocked front door swings open, pushed by a hungry child from the neighborhood who knows this family will love on him and feed him. Bobbie has flown in from Southern California for the camp, and now stands with arms folded across his chest, nodding.

The home represents so much more than walls, flooring, siding. There, a family overcame the hardest losses possible. They bonded together in grief and common commitment to live the kind of life their mother dreamt for them. The joyful sacrifices of that happy and hard season flit across all our minds.

We snap a picture together in front of their old house. Before we go our separate ways, I set the ball down, and gather everyone to pray for our families, this book, our health, and for Sugar's story to impact many lives for the sake of God's Kingdom. We clasp hands in our impromptu huddle.

Our Amen resounds. Immediately, the ball starts to roll down the hill towards the busy Fuller Avenue. Bobbie rushes down the hill for retrieval. Eyes wide, we stare at each other, realizing at the same time: that ball rolling down the hill is no accident.

Surely it is a sign of God's approval of this family, this book and His blessing upon all who will read it.

A story that began with a little four-year-old boy chasing after a basketball. Even though stopped in his tracks by a few balls to the chest, he still chases after his basketball dream. And so, we invite you, the reader of this book, to chase after your own God-given dreams. You may have the wind knocked out of you in the process, just as Sugar. But rather than being deterred, don't give up until you realize God's reasons and purposes for giving them to you. Keep chasing your dreams. As Sugar says, "You don't get what you don't fight for."

Those dreams may not turn out exactly as you expect. There may be twists and turns and detours along the way. But, as the author of your story, God would like nothing better than for you to realize the sweetness of the marvelous plans for your life that He had in mind when He formed you in your mother's womb. He will make your paths level. He will make it so the crooked lines turn straight. He will work all things together for your good.

The ball is in your court. Will you chase after your dreams with all your heart, soul, and mind, daring to be great rather than settling for just being good? If so, then I guarantee that your dreams will turn out as sweet as Sugar's. And you too will find yourself living the sweet life!

As Sugar says, "Play like the world is watching." Because the world *is* watching.

Sweet Dreams!

SWOOSH! ONE-ON-ONE WITH COACH VERN

SINCE I BEGAN THIS ADVENTURE, people have asked about my motivation for writing *Sweet Shot*. Sugar has been a bright light in my life since I first saw him play for Creston. I have a connection with Sugar for a variety of reasons, not just our love for basketball. Like Sugar, I tended to shoot from the outside for my points in games. People called me "Twig" growing up, since I had a similar body frame as Sugar's, so I could easily relate to his playing style on the court. Although, unlike Sugar, I was much more of a star in my mind than in actual games.

Also, being somewhat shy and easy-going, my temperament is similar to Sugar's. We are each the youngest child in our families. Neither of us is a stranger to loss. I didn't experience the death of my mom and one of my sisters until I was older. Still, the Wendt family experienced its own share of drama during my growing up years. Like Sugar, I would often escape to the basketball court for an outlet.

Finally, God has also used my love for basketball, along with my setbacks in the game, for greater good in my life. During elementary school, I dreamed of being a basketball star, and practiced hours on end to achieve that dream. By the time I

234 | Swoosh! One-on-One with Coach Vern

entered high school, I'd become a pretty good player. Some coaches I played for in the summer camps projected that I'd play Division I level basketball in college. However, prior to my freshman year in high school, East Grand Rapids hired a new head basketball coach, changing the dynamics of the team.

A year later, the new coach cut my brother Jamie from the varsity team along with several of his former JV teammates. His main focus, he told us, was on the class after us. His goal was to win the state championship and become a Division I college basketball coach. In spite of having winning teams and talented players, East hadn't won a state championship in basketball, since 1950.

Consequently, when I broke my wrist in practice early my sophomore year, I transferred to Grand Rapids Christian. I hoped for a better chance to soar with the Eagles. I put in long hours practicing for the upcoming season and thought I was fitting in well playing for Christian in the summer league. That summer, the Gus Macker Choo Choo Classic was held in Durand, Michigan. There in "The Railroad City, USA" I was even awarded the Division IV's Most Valuable Player.

When the tryouts began in November, I was all set to fly! Instead, I was grounded after being unexpectedly cut from the varsity team. Like Sugar, when he didn't see his name listed among the 1st Team All-Stars at the BC Camp, I could hardly believe my eyes. They began to fill with tears, when I didn't see my name on the team list. I was devastated!

Humiliated, I transferred back to East Grand Rapids the second semester of my junior year. During summer league ball, I felt confident that I had proved to our coach that I belonged on the varsity team. After I sank several shots in a scrimmage against Wyoming Rogers, he sat me down and personally told me he could use my outside shooting ability on the team. But something died in my spirit the day I was cut from Christian. I was so hurt that I didn't even play my senior year. Who knows?

Perhaps I could have contributed to our winning the 1982 Michigan High School Athletic Association Class B Boys Basketball State Championship? Last I checked, East Grand Rapids' High School still has only won one state championship in boys' basketball since it opened in 1917.

Yet, pain can be a pathway to a bigger and better plan. God in His Providence used this time of humiliation to draw me closer to Him and realize that He is the one thing I can depend upon, not basketball. I ended up coaching elementary school kids during my junior and senior years in high school. In college, I coached at Taylor University's summer basketball camp. There I used my basketball skills as a platform to share God's love in Christ Jesus with hundreds of kids. While coaching at Taylor, the Holy Spirit spoke to me about becoming a pastor.

A highlight of Sugar Mel's Basketball Camp is Dave Ginsberg's speech. When Gins called in sick during one of Sugar's camps, I was honored when Bobbie asked me to substitute. I'm no Dave Ginsberg, but I knew God had given me an opportunity to share what I learned about Sugar's secret of success. Join the campers of that Sweet Shot basketball camp as I share the gist of that speech.

SOME OF YOU MAY BE WONDERING, "Who is this guy speaking in front of you? Why is he here?"

I admit I didn't become the star basketball player I hoped to be when I was your age, but I still love the game of basketball. And my favorite player of all time is on the back of your T-shirt, Melvin Sugar McLaughlin.

He's the greatest long-range shooter I've ever seen. But it wasn't just what he did on the court, it was how he did it on and off the court, with style, class, and a smile. Here he is today, forty-plus years since I first saw him play, with the same love and passion for the game he had then—and the same love for people.

In getting to know Sugar, I have discovered the reason he became such a great basketball player. It's the same reason you can become a great basketball player, too. The same goes for anything else you want to achieve in life. Sugar sees basketball as a gift from God! As an expression of thanks to God, he is motivated to maximize that gift by being the best player possible.

What if you look to Sugar as a role model for you to not take the gifts God has given you for granted? And as an expression of thanks, maximize the gifts He has given you by always striving for greatness. Not just when it comes to playing basketball, but in all aspects of your life.

For example, when it comes to school, why not set the bar high for yourself and try to get a straight A report card, or make the honor roll? I've witnessed Sugar pulling individuals aside. He asks them, "Do you want to be great? Or do you just want to settle for being good? Then, you got to get your shots in! At least 500 shots a day in the summer and at least 200 shots a day during the season."

Ask yourself the same question in all the other areas of your life, as well: "Do you want to be great or do want to just settle for being good?" Then you got to give it your all!

Now if you didn't have the gifts for being great it'd be different. But I assure you that God has given you your own special gifts to be great in life! Never mind what others have or don't have. Instead, make it your goal to be the greatest version of yourself possible for God's glory!

As much as Sugar loves basketball, he's just as passionate about giving back to the community of Grand Rapids. That's why this camp exists. That's why God brought you here! Don't let Sugar down or all the people who have invested their time and energy in this camp. Don't let yourself down, by settling for anything less than your best, both on the court and off. Above all, don't let God down. We're counting on you!

I wasn't the basketball star I hoped I'd become. In hindsight, I know God answered my prayer in His own perfect way, by calling me into the ministry. Those basketball skills I practiced so hard to develop have been a platform for me to share God's love for us in Jesus with countless others wherever I've served. In His marvelously mysterious way, God has done something else amazing. He has made it possible for me to know the player I wanted to be like when I was growing up. What an honor to share his story through this book!

Dreams are worth fighting for, and reshaping in the fire of disappointment. Don't let your dream die in the midst of your refining. God loves you too much to fulfill your dream before you're ready. His delay does not mean His denial. He will often fulfill your dream in a way far more than you could ever ask or imagine. I promise you that. More than that, God does!

TWIG ALL-AMERICAN

FOR CHARLES J. NOVAK, JR.
NOVEMBER 26, 1952 – JANUARY 13, 2021

IN HONOR OF CHUCK NOVAK, friend, mentor, and hoops lover. His love for children motivated him to assist with *Sweet Shot*. He longed for its publication so younger readers could fulfill their God-given dreams.

Chuck now waits for Sugar and Vern to join him on heaven's playground.

"Blessed are the dead who die in the Lord from now on." "Yes," says the Spirit, "they will rest from their labor, for their deeds will follow them."
Rev. 14:13

ACKNOWLEDGMENTS

THIS BOOK IS A "DREAM COME TRUE," made possible by some special teammates God has blessed me with to bring it into reality. I thank God for:

My beloved "John 2" wife, Miran, who always challenges me to raise my game in everything I do. Truly, God has saved the best for last.

Sugar and Bobbie for entrusting me to tell their story, and opening their hearts and lives to me. Their love for each other reminds me of the brotherly love that I've been blessed to have with my own brother, Jamie.

Sugar's inner circle of family, friends, teammates, coaches, fans, and devoted followers for sharing their "Sugar stories." I trust that the stories that didn't make the cut for this book will be told and heard elsewhere.

My dad and mom, who showed me how to live by faith and not by sight.

My six older siblings who inspire me to greatness:

My oldest brother Dave, who I thought was the coolest person I knew growing up and still do. My brother Fred, who too often has sacrificed his own needs to take care of others, especially his youngest brother. My oldest sister, Kathy, for her drive and determination, especially after being hit by a drunk driver in her late twenties and incurring a closed head injury. My sister Beth, my November twin and fellow Engelein (little angel) for her kind, gentle spirit and listening ear. My sister Doralyn, who graduated from high school the same year as Sugar in 1979 and died of cancer at the age of fifty-five, whose inner beauty matched her outer beauty. My brother Jamie, for his support empathy, humor, and assessor of our similar pasts.

Jane Rubietta, my book coach, for her editing ability, counsel, expertise, and compassion.

Dave Ginsberg and Joe LaVoi for connecting me with some of the more difficult-to-reach interviewees and endorsers for this book.

Bryan Whitledge, the Archivist for Central Michigan University's Digital Records at the Clarke Historical Library.

Chuck Novak, a member at Messiah Lutheran Church in Chicago, who served as sounding board, grammarian, encourager, counselor, and friend; he lost the battle with brain cancer and has recently won the victory of heaven.

Brad Krause, also a member at Messiah, for his expertise in writing, photo editing, and design of *Sweet Shot*.

The rest of my members at Messiah Lutheran Church in Chicago for their prayers and support.

My best friend from Breton Downs Elementary School, Brian Gilmore for filming and recording some of the interviews during Sugar Mel's Sweet Shot camp in 2018.

My best friend from East Grand Rapids High School, Jim Cooper. God used him to help me enjoy life again after I was cut from the basketball team.

My best friend from Hope College, Caroline Atkinson (neé VanderKuy). Her prayers and devotion, together with my family's tireless love, helped restore me to health, mentally, physically, and spiritually, during a dark period in my life after I was hit by a car while running in Los Angeles in 2004.

Mrs. Pat Jackson, who has played the role of my black mother with her sage wisdom and counsel, ever since I was her pastor in the early 1990s.

The coaches in my life God has used to instill in me my love for sports, especially Mr. Richard Klunder (Hope Lutheran Church in Grand Rapids), Marion Crawley and Don Odle (Taylor University's Summer Basketball Camp). Ray McCahill (Aquinas College's Basketball Camp), Mark Howard (East Grand Rapids Junior High School); and Dr. William VanderBilt, my cross-country coach at Hope College.

Dave Odle and Coach Paul Patterson, for the privilege of working as a counselor/coach at Taylor University's Summer Basketball Camp in 1984 and 1985, even though I wasn't a star college player like some of the other counselors.

Derrick Wilkerson, who introduced my brother Jamie and me to black music and culture, as only a kid could to another kid in the '70s. Brant Wright (aka "Peanut"), who grew up in suburb similar to ours (Carmel, Indiana), and shared cross-cultural exchanges between Indiana and Michigan.

Mrs. Marva Collins, my favorite teacher at Breton Downs Elementary School, who kept my class picture on her wall as her all-time favorite student; and Mrs. Ann Mitchell, my favorite English teacher at East Grand Rapids High School for her enthusiasm for my writings.

Roeley Riendersma, our Dutch (OK, to be more specific Frisian) friend, who like Sugar's Dutch neighbor became part of our family and spoke with a cool accent.

The students, classmates, and coaches, during the years I attended East Grand Rapids High School and Grand Rapids Christian High School.

Our all time-favorite family dog, Brandy, who lived up to her AKC name, "Brandy, Sunshine of Andover," even though she chewed up my Most Valuable Player Gus Macker plaque when she was a puppy.

Above all, I owe my gratitude to the ultimate GOAT—The Triune God revealed in the inspired and inerrant Word of God. My Heavenly Father for loving me so much that He gave His only begotten Son to suffer and die on a cross for my sins. Because of this, I can be forgiven of all my sins and have eternal life in heaven. And for the Holy Spirit, who has called me by the Gospel and enlightens me with His gifts that I might live before God in righteousness and purity forever.

To God be the glory for the Great things He has done in providing me the support and encouragement of others to make this dream come true!

Soli Deo Gloria!

VEWJr.

ABOUT THE AUTHOR

Rev. Dr. Vernon E. Wendt Jr has been an ordained pastor in the Lutheran Church Missouri Synod since 1990. He has a Masters of Divinity and PhD in Missiology from Concordia Theological Seminary in Fort Wayne, Indiana.

He has served as a pastor and missionary in a wide variety of settings. His love for basketball has been a platform for him to share the Good News of Christ crucified for sinners. He has been an adjunct theology professor at Concordia University-Portland and Concordia University-Chicago, teaching bachelor's, master's and doctoral level courses. His doctoral dissertation "The Application of the Christian Faith by Small College Christian Athletes within the Sport of Basketball" was published by the University of Oregon's Microform Publications (2000).

Certified with Global Sports Chaplains with CEDE Sports, Vern has spoken on Christianity and Sports at college campuses throughout North America. He is a consultant for Christian athletic high school and college programs that seek to use sports as a witnessing tool, builder of character, and means of fostering community, while at the same time experiencing the freedom and play God intends for us to enjoy as His Kingdom people.

He's available to speak to athletes and athletic programs on cultivating a grace-based approach to sports. He loves helping people fully appreciate the joy of sports God has gifted us with. Plus, he can still demonstrate the proper form of shooting a jump shot. A technique that he worked hard to develop as an aspiring player! A former distance runner in college and marathon runner, he was hit by a car in Los Angeles in his late 30s. He's happy to be a plodder these days.

Vern is the proud founder of the Twig All-American Team, a selection of some of the top high school players in the country from the late 70s and early 80s. The TAA Team started around the same time as his friend John Perfitt's Perf All-American Team, and his brother Jamie's Flea-All-American Team. Melvin "Sugar" McLaughlin is Vern's top-rated Twig All-American of all time!

While his Macker Tournament play was the highlight of his so-called basketball career, it was also a lowlight when he experienced the agony of defeat on the Macker's main court in Lowell, Michigan. His brother Jamie had blown a wide-open lay-up that would have made the "Perf-Twig-Flea All-American Team" the first-place champions in their division! As an old man watching from inside the McNeal family garage bemoaned, "Oh, man! He could have put the game away!"

For more information and to invite Vern to your school, group, church, or team, see TwigAllAmerican.com. Email him at vern.wendt@TwigAllAmerican.com

TWIG ALL-AMERICAN

SUGAR MEL'S SWEET SHOT BASKETBALL CAMP

SUGAR MEL'S SWEET SHOT BASKETBALL CAMP is the oldest affordable camp in Grand Rapids, Michigan. It has been inspiring area youth to strive for greatness since 1993. In addition to Sugar, a first-rate staff offers knowledge, experience, and advice that campers can apply to improve their games. The lessons they learn apply not only to basketball. Besides that, they'll have a ball!

Sugar emphasizes to his campers, "I don't want you to settle for just being good. I want you to be great!" Thousands of young lives have been impacted by Sugar Mel's Camp. Not only has this resulted in them being better basketball players. Most importantly, it has influenced them to be better people.

Thanks to generous donations, students of all ages charge after their dreams, on and off the court. Your gift to Sugar Mel's Sweet Shot Basketball Camp, helps them guarantee that no children are turned away.

To register your child for camp, to volunteer, or to make a donation, visit SweetShotBasketballCamp.com. For even more information, call the camp at 616-222-6126 or email them at sugarmsm14@gmail.com.

Don't give up your God-given dreams!

Sugar Mel and Coach Vern team up to inspire audiences to greatness—both on and off the playing floor! Invite this dynamic duo to encourage your team, group, or league. Listeners will be challenged to give it their best shot, to live lives of purpose and meaning that will not only transform their own life but the lives of others.

@sugarmelbasketballcamp
SweetShotBasketballCamp.com
https://www.facebook.com/SugarMelBasketballCamp

NOTES

1. Living the Sweet Life

1. Rose White, "Students from over 60 countries graduate from East Kentwood High School," *wzzm13.com*, May 26, 2019, accessed October 25, 2020, https://www.wzzm13.com/article/news/education/students-from-over-60-countries-graduate-from-east-kentwood-high-school/69-5d10eef2-d1c9-468e-b219-fea2d151becc.
2. "The race is not to the swift or the battle to the strong, nor does food come to the wise or wealth to the brilliant or favor to the learned; but time and chance happen to them all." Eccles. 9:11, NIV.

2. Two Soon, Two Late

1. Bill Simmons, *The Book Of Basketball: The NBA According to The Sports Guy* (New York, NY: Ballantine Books, 2009), 139–142.
2. Terry Pluto, *Loose Balls: The Short, Wild Life Of The American Basketball Association* (New York: Simon & Schuster Paperbacks, 1990), 70.
3. Steve Kaminski, "All-time greats: Melvin 'Sugar' McLaughlin is Grand Rapids' best player ever," *Michigan Live,* February 23, 2016, accessed August 30, 2020, https://www.mlive.com/sports/grand-rapids/2016/02/all-time_greats_melvin_sugar_m.html.
4. Evan Petzold, "The story of Melvin 'Sugar' McLaughlin, and Presley Hudson breaking his all-time scoring record," *Central Michigan Life,* February 13, 2019, accessed August 30, 2020, http://www.cm-life.com/article/2019/02/melvin-sugar-mclaughlin-central-michigan-basketball-presley-hudson-chippewas-breaking-all-time-scoring-record-dick-parfitt-johnny-orr-jim-boyce-story

3. Call Him Sugar

1. Gary Johnson, "OLLIE MCLAUGHLIN," *Michigan Rock and Roll Legends,* June 1, 2018, accessed August 30, 2020, https://michiganrockandrolllegends.com/index.php/mrrl-hall-of-fame/366-ollie-mclaughlin .

2. "Last Names MCLAUGHLIN," *My Name Stats*, accessed August 30, 2020, http://www.mynamestats.com/Last-Names/M/MC/MCLAUGHLIN/index.html.
3. "Former New Mexico State star dead at 60," *AP News*, January 23, 1997, accessed August 30, 2020, https://apnews.com/65f49c1a6e9279d4c7e2441f913452a6.
4. Kaminski, "All-time greats: Melvin 'Sugar' McLaughlin is Grand Rapids' best player ever," (see ch 2, n.4).
5. Mike Lloyd, "Black artist struggles to secure minorities a spot on comic page." *The Grand Rapids Press*, May 29, 1988. 7-D.
6. Jim Knight, "'Sugar' packet nets an award, *Central Michigan Life*, June 22, 1983, accessed August 30, 2020, cmuhistory.cmich.edu/?a=d&d=Isabella-CML19830622.1.13&srpos=1&e=-------en-10--1--txt-txIN-sugar packets ----- .

4. Love at First Bounce

1. Kaminski, "All-time greats: Melvin 'Sugar' McLaughlin is Grand Rapids' best player ever," (see ch 2, n.4).

5. Fun, Laughter, and Music in Ann Arbor

1. Gary Johnson, "OLLIE MCLAUGHLIN" https://michiganrockandrolllegends.com/index.php/mrrl-hall-of-fame/366-ollie-mclaughlin
2. Ibid.
3. Ibid.
4. Ibid.
5. Dave Moore, "Ollie McLaughlin," 2005. Retrieved from https://web.archive.org/web/20200202232043/www.hitsvillesoulclubs.com/olliemclaughlin.htm
6. "Ollie McLaughlin," *Wikipedia,* July 9, 2018, accessed August 30, 2020, https://en.wikipedia.org/wiki/Ollie_McLaughlin.
7. Susan Wineberg, "Demolition of Houses throughout Ann Arbor Destroy a Piece of History as Well," *The Ann Arbor News,* January 26, 2013, comment by Thaddeus, January 27, 2013, accessed August 30, 2020, www.annarbor.com/news/opinion/demolition-of-houses-throughout-ann-arbor-destroy-a-piece-of-history-as-well/.
8. Gary Johnson, "OLLIE MCLAUGHLIN."

6. Home Court Advantage in Grand Rapids

1. Will Mack, "Grand Rapids Uprising (1967)," *Black Past,* January 13, 2018, accessed February 27, 2020, http://www.blackpast.org/african-american-history/1967-grand-rapids-uprising-1967/

2. Monica Scott, "'I wanted to fight back': Reflections on the 1967 Grand Rapids riot," *MLive,* July 18, 2017, last modified May 20, 2019, accessed August 31, 2020, https://www.mlive.com/news/grand-rapids/2017/07/i_thought_i_was_dead_memories.html

3. "A History of the Civil Rights Movement in Grand Rapids, Michigan," accessed August 31, 2020 http://www.arcgis.com/apps/MapJournal/index.html?appid=0642f76537354f3982b58f09ed514932

4. "Roughly 4,000 people were displaced from highway construction through Grand Rapids: An interview with Fr. Dennis Morrow," *Grand Rapids People's History Project,* March 4, 2016, accessed August 31, 2020, https://grpeopleshistory.org/2016/03/04/roughly-4000-people-were-displaced-from-highway-construction-through-grand-rapids-an-interview-with-fr-dennis-morrow/

5. Chris Ballard, The Great Lakes Region, in *Hoops Nation: A Guide to America's Best Pickup Basketball* (New York, NY: Henry Holt and Company, 1998), 217-248.

6. Greg Johnson, "Grand Rapids Homecomings Are Always Sweet for 'Sugar'." *The Grand Rapids Press*, April 16, 1983, p. 1C.

7. Steve Kaminski, "All-time greats: Legacy of underdog Don 'The Animal' Edwards lives on half-century later," *MLive,* February 22, 2016, last modified April 3, 2019, accessed August 31, 2020, https://www.mlive.com/sports/grand-rapids/2016/02/all-time_greats_legacy_of_unde.html

8. Peter J. Wallner, "Former Ottawa Hills and Michigan basketball player Ernie Johnson dies," *Michigan Live,* February 15, 2018, last modified January 30, 2019, accessed August 31, 2020, https://www.mlive.com/sports/grand-rapids/2018/02/former_ottawa_hills_and_michig_2.html .

9. Stacy Ladenburger, "Planting Seeds and Singing Songs: In Celebration of 40 Years of Faithful Service," Bax50, http://www.wearebaxter.org/whoweare/

10. "Paul Phillips," Central High School Foundation, accessed August 31, 2020, http://chsfomaha.org/news-4/860-paul-phillips

11. Reinder Van Til, Gordon L Olson, et al, *Thin Ice: Coming of Age in Grand Rapids,* "Wilma, Whitey, and the Tackers," by William Brashler, (Grand Rapids, MI: Wm. B. Eerdmans Publishing, 2007), 256-268.

12. "Delton Heard Obituary," *Pittsburgh Post-Gazette, April 8, 2003*. accessed August 31, 2020, https://www.legacy.com/obituaries/postgazette/obituary.aspx?n=delton-a-heard&pid=920409

13. "ADDIX Basketball Champions All-Star Classic Set For March 29," March 20, 2017, accessed August 31, 2020, https://dupanthers.com/news/

2017/3/20/womens-basketball-addix-basketball-champions-all-star-classic-set-for-march-29.aspx

14. Jason Hutton, "All Star basketball games to honor TA-WA-SI," June 10, 2019, accessed June 8, 2020, from https://fox17online.com/2019/06/10/all-star-games-to-honor-ta-wa-si/

7. Sweet Shot

1. Timothy Ferris, *The 4-Hour Chef* (New York, NY: Houghton Mifflin Harcourt Publishing Company, 2012) 596-599.
2. Michael E. Smith, "McLaughlin Set for Winning Year," *Central Michigan Life*, December 3, 1982, 12.
3. Al-Din, ibid, ch. 6 n. 37.

9. Finding a Refuge in Basketball

1. Chuck Wieglus and Alexander Wolfff, "Going Courting," *The In-Your-Face-Basketball Book* (Pickering, Ontario: Beaverbooks, 1980) 19-37.
2. Bob Becker, "I'll take mine with Some 'Sugar'," *The Grand Rapids Press*, May 25, 2008, 5-D.
3. Becker, ibid.

10. It Takes a Team to Raise a Player

1. Brian VanOchten, "Sweet Day For 'Sugar'," *The Grand Rapids Press*, January 17, 1999, 11-E.
2. VanOchten, ibid.
3. Joseph J. Hulsebus,"GRAND RAPIDS Tackers," February 26, 2006, accessed August 31, 2020, http://www.semiprofootball.org/gtackers.htm
4. William Powell, "Herschell Turner turns back the clock and shares his story of Art and Hoops," Keeping the Nostalgia Alive! Show. June 11, 2018, accessed August 31, 2020, https://radiopublic.com/keeping-the-nostalgia-alive-show-GApj5N/s1!2ca83
5. Brashler, *Thin Ice,* ibid.
6. Doug Tribou,"Grand Rapids resident Minnie Forbes is part of Negro Leagues baseball history," NPR Michigan Radio, February 24, 2020, accessed August 31, 2020, https://www.michiganradio.org/post/grand-rapids-resident-minnie-forbes-part-negro-leagues-baseball-history
7. "Player Interviews: Highlights of Interviews with Former Negro League Players," Center for Negro League Baseball, accessed August 31, 2020, http://www.cnlbr.org/Portals/0/RL/Player Interviews.pdf

8. Peter J. Wallner, "Rasberry Field dedicated: 'He would have thought this was something'," *The Grand Rapids Press*, May 26, 2016, 3-C.

9. Josh Slagter, "Grand Rapids Public Schools athletic director Melvin Atkins retiring with the City League," Michigan Live, March 6, 2008, accessed August 31, 2020, https://www.mlive.com/grpress/2008/03/grand_rapids_public_schools_at.html

10. Slagter, "Mel Atkins," ibid.

11. Steve Kaminski, "OK Conference commissioner Jim Haskins stepping down," Michigan Live, last modified April 2, 2018, accessed August 31, 2020, https://www.mlive.com/sports/grand-rapids/2018/03/ok_conference_commissioner_jim.html

12. Peter J. Wallner, "Grand Rapids Sports Hall of Fame date and ticket price announced," *Michigan Live,* last modified January 30, 2019, accessed Sept. 2, 2020, https://www.mlive.com/sports/grand-rapids/2018/07/grand_rapids_sports_hall_of_fa_15.html

13. Melvin McLaughlin, SugarMel Bball Summer Camp, *Facebook,* August 7, 2017, accessed September 2, 2020, https://www.facebook.com/SugarMelBasketballCamp/videos/vb.100006123725197/1972162592997846/?type=2&video_source=user_video_tab

11. Middle School Phenom

1. Scott Scholten, "McLaughlin Threatened City Record," *The Grand Rapids Press*, March 4, 1978, 3B.

12. Shooting Star for the Polar Bears

1. Brent Ashcroft, "'The Spirit of South High': 50 years after closing, legendary school still teaches," WZZM13, last modified May 25, 2018, accessed September 2, 2020, https://www.wzzm13.com/article/news/local/michigan-life/the-spirit-of-south-high-50-years-after-closing-legendary-school-still-teaches/69-556594440

2. Natalie Hart, "Grand Rapids Pastors Explore the History of Our Education System," G-RAP, October 31, 2016, accessed September 2, 2020, https://www.grpastors.org/blog/the-one-about-education

3. Higgins v. BOARD OF EDUCATION, GRAND RAPIDS, MICH., 395 F. Supp. 444 (W.D. Mich. 1973), JUSTIA US Law, July 18, 1973, accessed September 2, 2020, https://law.justia.com/cases/federal/district-courts/FSupp/395/444/1416359/

4. Dan Nilsen, "City League: Patient Union Press Finally Pays Off," *The Grand Rapids Press,* January 15, 1977, 1B.

5. Dan Nilsen, "City League: Creston Puts on Another Awesome Show In Rolling Over West Catholic, 92-63," *The Grand Rapids Press*, January 22, 1977, 1B.

6. Scott Scholten, "Fatigued Creston Reaches 'A' Final." *The Grand Rapids Press*, March 3, 1977, 9-B.

7. Roger D. Hart, "CMU Signs All-Stater," *Central Michigan Life*, April 18, 1978, 17.

8. Scott Scholten, "Union's 4th-Quarter Blitz Beats Creston," *The Grand Rapids Press*, December 3, 1977, 1B.

9. Corky Meinecke, "Central Wins Title With 2-Game Bulge," *The Grand Rapids Press*, February 25, 1978, 2-B.

10. Art Preuss, "Melvin Shreds the Nets, Bears Nip Norris," *The Grand Rapids Press,* November 25, 1978, 1- B.

11. Bob Becker, "Orr Sees Just How Sweet It Is," *The Grand Rapids Press*, December 20, 1978, 1D–3D.

12. Alan Whitt, "Scott Gives Creston Depth for City Chase," *The Grand Rapids Press*, February 3, 1979, 1-B.

13. Len Painter, "Coach Al returns to GH to reminisce about Buc basketball," PAINTER (blog), July31, 2012, *www.grandhaventribune.com*. Retrieved from https://www.grandhaventribune.com/opinion/blogs/painter-coach-al-returns-to-gh-to-reminisce-about-buc-basketball/article_ebca5dbe-4a0c-52db-8b8a-5052b1af9d5e.html

14. Leo Martonosi, "Creston's McLaughlin puts on show in Civic Center," *Holland Sentinel*, March 3, 1979, 20.

15. Ruth Butler, "Presenting the Best on The Grand Rapids Press Prep Team," *The Grand Rapids Press*, April 1, 1979, 1-J.

16. Terry Foster, "Missing Links: Parfitt Needs to fill vacancies left by departed seniors," *Central Michigan Life*, August 27, 1979, 12C.

17. Steve Kaminski, "All-time greats: Melvin 'Sugar' McLaughlin is Grand Rapids' best player ever," *Michigan Live,* last modified April 3, 2019, accessed September 2, 2020, https://www.mlive.com/sports/grand-rapids/2016/02/all-time_greats_melvin_sugar_m.html

18. Scott Scholten, "McLaughlin Outscores Big Brother But Rice Diet Proves Too Rich," *The Grand Rapids Press*, December 28, 1977, p. 7-B.

19. Alan Whitt, "Creston Left in the Dark," *The Grand Rapids Press*, December 29, 1978, 15-A.

20. Ruth Butler, "Falcon Stall Can't Stop The Bears," *The Grand Rapids Press*, February 12, 1978, 3-B.

21. Kaminski, "All-time greats," ibid.

13. Sweet Memories of a Shining Star

1. The Scoreboard, *The Grand Rapids Press*, January 6, 1979, 4B.
2. Steve Kaminski, "Grand Rapids Creston athletics: Thanks for the memories," last modified August 22, 2019, accessed September 2, 2020, https://www.mlive.com/highschoolsports/article/grand-rapids-creston-athletics-thanks-for-the-memories/
3. Kaminski, ibid.
4. Alan Whitt, "Tournament Time Means End of the Line for Some Stars," *The Grand Rapids Press*, February 28, 1979, 3D.

15. Can Any Good Basketball Player Come out of Grand Rapids?

1. Scott Scholten, "Grand Rapids High Schools Lack Basketball Assembly Line." *The Grand Rapids Press*, April 19, 1978, 3-D.
2. Scott Scholten, ibid.
3. Mick McCabe, "Michigan Preps Make Mincemeat of Yugoslavs 'Imposters'," *Detroit Free Press*, April 24, 1979, 36.
4. "Melvin Displays 'D' As Respect Mounts For State Basketball," *The Grand Rapids Press*, April 8, 1979, 2-J.
5. Alan Whitt, "Michigan Stars Fall in Finals," *The Grand Rapids Press*, April 9, 1979, pp. 1-D.
6. "Melvin Displays 'D'," 2-J.
7. "B/C: WHEN IT BEGAN," B/C All-Stars Basketball, accessed September 2, 2020, http://bcallstarsbasketball.net/photos/index.htm
8. THE B/C Story, ibid.
9. "B/C: WHEN IT BEGAN," ibid.
10. "HER F CE IS F MILI R," B/C All-Stars Basketball, accessed September 2, 2020, http://www.bcallstarsbasketball.net/history.htm
11. B/C All Stars 1978 Basketball Camps, November 1, 1978, accessed September 2, 2020, http://www.bcallstarsbasketball.net/history_sports_stories.htm.
12. B/C All Stars 1978 Basketball Camp, November 1, 1978, accessed September 2, 2020, http://www.bcallstarsbasketball.net/history_sports_stories.htm.

16. Loyalty Wins Sugar for the Chippewas

1. Alan Whitt, "McCarter Completes Swift Rise to Top," *The Grand Rapids Press,* April 11, 1979, 1-C.

2. Petzold, "The story of Melvin 'Sugar' McLaughlin, and Presley Hudson breaking his all-time scoring record."
3. Petzold, ibid.
4. Hart, "CMU signs All-Stater," 19.
5. Alan Whitt, "Parfitt Gets Melvin's Autograph, Is Sky High," *The Grand Rapids Press*, April 18, 1979, 3-D.
6. "Koger signs basketball letter," *Central Michigan Life*, May 7, 1979, 12.

17. Firing Up for the Chips: "Oh, My!"

1. Evan Petzold, "Hudson Makes History," *Central Michigan Life*, February 21, 2019, 12–13.
2. Terry Foster, "Deja Vu! Chip win sweet as 'Sugar'," *Central Michigan Life*, January 28, 1980, 9.
3. Jean Spenner, "BG down, Hurons to go," *Central Michigan Life*, February 22, 1980, 8.
4. Petzold, "Hudson Makes History," 12–13.
5. Scott Heitman, "McLaughlin, Knuckles named to All-MAC basketball squad," *Central Michigan Life*, March 18, 1981,16.
6. Petzold, "Hudson Makes History," 12–13.
7. Petzold, "Hudson Makes History," 12–13.
8. "Opposing coaches comment on the senior sensation," *Centralight*, January 1983, 2.
9. Scott Heitman, "Chips explode, 103-87; travel to OU," *Central Michigan Life*, February 6, 1981, 10.
10. Matt Dobek, "Cagers' recovery comes too late," *Central Michigan Life*, February 20, 1981, 8.
11. "Melvin picked league's best," *Central Michigan Life*, February 4, 1981, 15.
12. "Opposing coaches comment," *Centralight*, January 1983, p. 2.
13. "Opposing coaches comment," 2.
14. John Burdick, "Cagers surprise Huskies in an upset," *Central Michigan Life*, January 22, 1982, 8.
15. John Burdick, "Sweetness! McLaughlin is MAC's best," *Central Michigan Life*, March 16, 1982, 16.
16. "Cagers honored," *Central Michigan Life*, March 10, 1982, 13.
17. Jon Becker, "McLaughlin set for MAC title race," *Centralight*, Janauary 1983, 2.
18. Becker, "McLaughlin set," 2.
19. Petzold, "Hudson Makes History," 12-13.
20. Craig Bon, "Seeking sweet success," *Chippewa Yearbook* (Mount Pleasant, MI: Central Michigan University, 1983), 272.
21. Bon, "Seeking sweet success," 272.

22. Bob Becker, "Melvin Goes Out With His Guns Blazing," *The Grand Rapids Press*, March 3, 1983, D1.
    Chapter 17: Embracing the Central Spirit
23. "CBS gets film," *Central Michigan Life*, April 1, 1983, 8.
24. "NCAA Men's Final Four Rankings Hub," *Sports Media Watch*, accessed October 28, 2020, https://www.sportsmediawatch.com/ncaa-final-four-ratings-history-most-watched-games-cbs-tbs-nbc/

18. Embracing the Central Spirit

1. Larry G. Owens, "CMU Makes a Great Choice: Coles to Replace Parfitt," *The Grand Rapids Press,* March 20, 1985, 5E.

19. Sugar's Dream Turns Sour

1. Bob Becker, "Can Sugar Sweeten Sour Cavs?" *The Grand Rapids Press*, June 29, 1983, 2C.
2. Jeff Stroble, Joseph Rebholz, Drew Crossley, Nathan Milliron, Jeffrey McCutchan, Dave Adkins, and Michael Uporsky, comments on Fun While It Lasted, Continental Basketball Association (1978-2009) April 27, 2020, accessed September 3, 2020, https://funwhileitlasted.net/continental-basketball-association-1978-2009/
3. Bill Collison, "Spirits sign 'Sugar' McLaughlin," *Detroit Free Press*, October 27, 1983, 2D.
4. "Spirits Obtain McLaughlin," *Central Michigan Life*, October 31, 1983, 10.
5. Steve Kowalski, "Sugar Overcomes Cuts," *Central Michigan Life*, January 30, 1984, 9.
6. Kowalski, "Sugar Overcomes," 9.
7. Kowalski, "Sugar Overcomes," 9.

20. A Baller for Life

1. Gary Bond, "It's no wonder this team still wins," *The Grand Rapids Press,* April 11, 1991, 1C.
2. "McLaughlin leads Debut to state title," *The Grand Rapids Press*, April 2, 1990, 1D–7D.
3. Bob Becker, "Do Hoops need a Sugar shot?" *The Grand Rapids Press*, October 27, 1990, 1C.
4. "Melvin Sugar McLaughlin," accessed September 3, 2020, https://macker.com/news/post/melvin-sugar-mclaughlin

5. Bob Becker, "'Sugar' gets a shot to play on Magic's team," *The Grand Rapids Press*, November 16, 1993, 1D.
6. Becker, "'Sugar' gets a shot," 1D.
7. Ibid.
8. Ibid.
9. Ibid.
10. Leo Martonisi, "Hoop legend scores 68 points," *The Holland Sentinel*, August 24, 2009, 9A.

21. Sweet Shot Gives Back to the Community

1. Brian VanOchten, "Majerle shines brightest in all-star win," *The Grand Rapids Press,* July 24, 1993, C-1.
2. UBEM, HAAWK Publishing, CMRRA, LatinAutor – UMPG, UMPG Publishing, LatinAutor, ASCAP, and 5 Music Rights Societies SHOW LESS. ([SixMixtapeAlot] (2018, August 6). La The Darkman – Swisha and Dosha (Feat. Willie The Kid) [Living Notoriously]. https://www.youtube.com/watch?v=LygC9i_RhaU